I AM I

The Indweller of Your Heart

BOOK TWO

Also by David Knight

Pathway

Deliverance of Love, Light and Truth

I am I: The Indweller of Your Heart—Book One

I am I: The Indweller of Your Heart—Book Three

I am I: The Indweller of Your Heart—'Collection'

Leave the Body Behind—Sojourns of the Soul

A Pocket Full of God

I AM I

The Indweller of Your Heart

BOOK TWO

52 LESSONS TO HELP YOU FIND THE JOY AND BLISS OF BEING 'YOU'

David Knight

If you enjoy reading *I AM I The Indweller of Your Heart*—**Book Two**
—you can find further inspiring and motivation books when you join
David's mission for a 'full and blissful life'.

To learn more, visit www.AscensionForYou.com
and download ***Deliverance of Love, Light and Truth*** for free.

ACKNOWLEDGMENTS

To God, for the privilege bestowed upon me, in receiving these words of wisdom, knowledge and peace ... for this book has created yet another steppingstone towards the eternal love and bliss which is within us all.

To all guides and teachers from within God's light hierarchy, who have truly given and shared their love so freely, making my life (and heart) so rich and complete, that mere words cannot begin to describe how I feel.

I wish to thank my wife Caroline in recognition of her support, patience and love, Rachael Hardcastle and Nathan Dasco for their creativity and for the encouragement of all past and present members of the Peterborough Sai Baba group ... and my family and friends who are so special to me too.

MAY GOD BLESS YOU ALL

TABLE OF CONTENTS

FOREWORD

This may be the first time that you have set eyes upon this book or, having read part one, you will have become familiar with how and why these words fall upon each page. You read them because you are being guided to do so.

Regarding your own spiritual development, it is time to live and become who and what you truly are. Please understand, you are love; you are light, and you are everything—all-powerful, brilliant, and majestic—and you will soon be able to move forward and experience your own divinity … and also display one's divine essence for others to sense, feel, and share too.

In fact, through knowledge and experience, you will gain wisdom, where you can shine and resonate with positive thoughts, words, and deeds.

So, may your journey be full of joy, with your hopes and dreams fulfilled, knowing you are part of 'creation'. Remember, while you re-learn the truth —with the aid of these lessons—try to live and share the life you have always wanted to create … both for yourself and for many others, too.

LESSON 1:

FREEDOM

David, you will always know when to write, because you sense and 'realise' me in your heart ... where our connection remains forever. Indeed, all life that exists—including the dimensions of time and space—are linked, so there is no separation or division, as we are 'one'.

Thoughts—regarding the structure of this new lesson—flash through your consciousness, but do not concern yourself over this. You will know when and where to place it in this book. Such details are not so important within the grander scheme of things ... inconsequential, you might say.

In fact, people become overly concerned with 'time', and those minutes, hours, days, weeks, and years, because of the way the physical body lives upon the 'earth-plane'. Therefore, always try to live in the moment, the present (pre-sent), in terms of love within your hearts.

Please understand, I do not mean for you to forget or attempt to erase the past, or even dismiss one's future days of growth and maturity as a human being. Know that when you can focus upon the 'moment', you ease the burden of your mind, which constantly tries to trick you. We will discuss this in a short while.

You noticed that when I first asked you to pick up the pen — by the love that connects us pulling upon your heart—you did not write the words 'Hello David'. This is because it would show we have been apart, as if two friends were re-communicating. This, of course, would be untrue. As I just stated, we are 'one', and I am you and you are me.

Those who are awakening from the sleep of doubt will soon understand this. Any soul who currently lies within shadow—as if under a parasol upon a sunny day—will gradually be able to expand and breathe in more light.

This trepidation, confusion, and any misunderstanding of your purpose concerning physical embodiment are strange but true. Resembling a snare or trap, the environment around a person seems to prohibit them from seeking, searching, grasping, and comprehending the truth, both within and out. For these reasons, the title of this lesson should now make more sense.

It is quite clear that people often depict freedom as being free from persecution and hatred, or to live in a democratic society. Well, this may be correct, but how true are they? If you consider there are 'rules' to follow and various legislations to be obeyed upon the lands of the Earth—set by governments—this can lead to fear … not only from the state, but from other people, and even fearing oneself!

From the condition of one's mind, and the ability to roam where you choose, would this imply you are actually free? Those incarcerated—for whatever reason by law—or if one appears trapped by circumstance and even the forces of nature, then you might believe this. Yet the aforementioned statement would still be accurate and true.

Similarly, for those who cannot see, would you think blindness is a so-called disability and a hindrance to everyday life? Someone who can bear witness to a beautiful flower, rainbow, mountain, or the brightness of the sun shimmering upon a lake may say it is, However, the blind 'man' is not tempted by what his mind sees, and then thinks he needs. There is no desire. No wanting or wishing. Compare these two scenarios and think of who is totally free.

Prejudice and human frailty assume those without one or more of the senses are imperfect or even useless. Do not succumb to these thoughts or feelings. Only on a physical plane of existence do you encounter such traits. Upon all other levels of energy and vibration, their influence is not so apparent or even required. Self-realization brings wholeness and verifies one is complete and eternal.

Realise the body is a mask, hiding what lies beneath. It is only when your true abilities as a soul 'shine' that the exterior peels away. This reveals such beauty and peace. It becomes easier to recognize who, what, and why you are—divine.

Please do not consider your own body as ugly, misshapen, somehow incorrect, or even hopeless. It is precious and required and enables you to achieve what you were 're-born' to do and be. I urge you to protect, cherish, and understand this casing of your soul. I will never criticize how you live your life, as those decisions are yours alone to make.

Comprehend that you tire as you age … and will become unable to accomplish things as easily as an adolescent or a young adult. Proof indeed, your physical 'energy' dissipates like a battery or cell. However, unlike its core, your divinity remains as powerful and bright as you wish it to be.

Therefore, are you illuminated? Or is your brightness kept hidden behind a shadow of fear and doubt? Like a torch under a blanket, you may see everything close around you, but those on the outside visualise only shades of uncertainty. This is not your actual light, so you must appreciate this and show you are already free. Hence, my gift today is to re-empower and help you recognize what is reality. I will recharge your life and wishes and dreams, in order for you to fulfil your true goal of self-realization and liberation.

Appreciate you are all full of negatives and positives. Therefore, I aim to bring balance back into your lives. Consider me the touch paper, the conduit and the connection which combine and link the circle of truth together, and unlike those batteries which are discarded from one's home appliances, you will always remain powerful and strong.

Know too, it does not matter whether the physical is burnt, buried or frozen, because once your consciousness and light has departed, through so-called 'death'—and as long as it has served its purpose—only you can decide what takes place next. You may consider your soul as being free from the attachment of the body. This lack of restriction is what you deserve and inherit, and it becomes your soul's decision whether to journey back into a new 'embodiment'. Woven into the fabric of your being, resides this choice to become even brighter … and shine like the star you truly ought to be.

Understand, one's embodiment can take countless forms in many places of time and space, because everything is connected. Hence, all dimensions … no matter how, where, and why they exist, are all there for souls to develop and to attain their ascension. Do not be disheartened … or imagine 'freedom'—in every sense of the word—is unattainable. In addition, do not misunderstand that being free represents 'Heaven' either. This is only being what you, I and 'all' life already is ... the love, light, and truth.

Always be yourself. Try not to be the one who disguises him or herself, projecting false thoughts or pain upon another. This only captivates and traps another soul, misleading them, and removes the very freedom you all seek. Therefore, please shine your love from deep within so others can bask in the true light form of your being. Be kind and forgiving at every opportunity, even when you think another does not deserve it.

You are all magnificent, beautiful, and amazing, too. Of course, these are merely words. No such language or verbal expression can ever depict or explain true love. One only needs to observe those hearts and eyes when they meet for the first time. For example, the lovers, the partners, or a future husband and wife.

It is knowing and accepting—to the core of your divinity—that you feel something is right for you. In this moment of happiness … within companionship and friendship, the beauty of two hearts becoming one is where you sense 'freedom' from all cares, worries and concerns. This is joy beyond all joy, peace beyond all peace, and this 'oneness' lies ahead in eternity. It is priceless beyond everything. This is true freedom, and it lives in both you and me forever. Amen.

LESSON 2:

BODY, MIND, AND SOUL

Truth flows to, through, and from every heart at all times and places. Though this is fact—which goes hand in hand with love and enables all life to exist—most of humankind does not perceive or understand this.

Does this mean there is some sort of dividing line between the lives of those who can and those who cannot? No, because where and how could this ever occur? Could a wall, fence, or any other barrier be created high enough for segregation? Can land, sea, or air prevent the movement and travel of thoughts, hopes, or dreams of a single man, woman, or child?

In reality, only the inner development of a being can deny, renounce, or inhibit the kindness, peace, and purity of the mind or body and the soul. So, are those who think or feel this way less worthy of my love? Of course not, because I would endorse some self-inflicted harm upon myself.

Therefore, in order to expand your own light, please comprehend and acknowledge our 'oneness'. One must appreciate and apply this to all their thoughts, words, and deeds. It will seem strange to contemplate what you say, think or do as having many consequences beyond your immediate surroundings, but you need to realise this is true.

Consider any aspect of parenthood, or even the education of a child. It becomes easier to appreciate their upbringing—how being guided by their mother, father and teachers, particularly through the early years—will profoundly influence both conduct and character throughout their life. A responsibility is therefore bestowed upon both pupil and the 'guide', to ensure one's growth of both heart and mind whilst on the 'earth-plane'.

Remember, such words and actions do not affect the soul in your physical form. It is 'free' from prejudice, hatred, anguish, or pain of any kind. Only during physical embodiment do such issues become apparent, because they reflect within and on your bodily 'condition'.

One may consider or think about a multitude of concerns or problems, perhaps an illness, disease or condition that not only annoys or angers, but frustrates or even dictates how, where, and why you live your life the way you do. Of course, any ailment could be 'inherited'; and some people describe these as passing down through one's DNA or 'being in your genes'. Indeed, these links over many generations can produce these effects, but are they random in nature, or your own fate to endure?

Please know, whatever condition and abilities you think you do—or do not possess—or even can or cannot use, you are perfect. You are whole. It is but a fleeting moment, and a fragment of your so-called 'time' upon the Earth, which needs accepting and tolerating.

Some will now point out or say that if I am truly God, then why does there need to be suffering of any kind? Why should a child be ill or in pain? You may also know someone who says of another, "He (or she) do so much good for the local community and our society, so why do they suffer so much? It is not right or fair."

Please do not become enclosed by any train of thought or contained within a box, as there is no such thing. Remember, love is truth and faultless, and at your core you are the same, because of our totality. Understandably, when a person or animal is suffering—particularly with bodily pain—it is natural they want this to end, and who would not want to be pain free?

Many people, though, will not complain to family, friends or even their peers, because they find it easier to accept and appreciate a process has begun. Perhaps, in their acknowledgement of what's taking place, they realise this is still temporary, even if there have been many years of anguish.

You often hear that 'true wealth is your health', and therefore it is important to understand if you are healthy, you have an advantage and the ability to conquer those worldly desires, which try to hinder and prevent you from knowing the truth of who, what, and why you 'are' with greater ease.

Of course, it is easy for someone not in any pain to criticize or diminish these times as being an annoyance or a nuisance, often inciting another person to overcome such things and, "just get on with it". Perhaps guilt—or even frustration—then plays its part.

Again, I will not disapprove or chastise any of you. I only wish you to do the best you can in all areas of your life. This way not only are you true to others, but also to yourself. Then, by living in truth, strands of love and light multiply and expand beyond your four walls to connect and touch hearts and minds and souls you cannot even imagine. In doing so, a resonance of peace, harmony and bliss will emanate from, through and to all things.

Understand it is vital to control your thoughts too, so do not let them dictate to you, as the mind is not the real you ... 'you' are 'outside' of the mind. This is simple to comprehend, because if you realize you are thinking of something, then you are separate from it. Separation allows you to determine when and how this tries to inflict false desires.

Remember, you will often associate these thoughts as wants or needs, usually with the material or physical world around you. I am not implying everything you observe, and view is bad for you, but you should use your intuition and use discernment in the acceptance of such.

Contentment, too, will also play a huge part in meeting the mind's often-wayward role head on. When you are content, you become a happier and most amiable person, which filters through the very fabric of your home and surroundings, as well as the conduct of yourself as a human being.

Know I love you in all situations, whether one is in poverty or rich beyond your wildest dreams, though only those who live in these respective scenarios can say if they are content or not. Monetary riches cannot buy you love and never will; it can make you feel more comfortable and may even give you the ability to make choices of where you can live, but this will never show you how to live.

Money and the 'material' can indeed influence people (and the world), in what they think of you, but they can never disguise the inner you from me. Appearances count for nothing in love and truth, for it is your character and personality that depicts the light emanating from your soul, as I explained so many times before.

For instance, do those who live in real poverty and destitution wish they had the latest sports car or large diamond ring on their finger? No, for if they were hungry or thirsty, these things would not even enter their consciousness or mind … it only fixed their thoughts upon food or water.

Appreciate the perception and realities are those reflections of both shadow and light. Often, these are believed to be those so-called 'good and bad' events a person incurs, when in fact they are simply the experiences of the soul. With this knowledge—and by what takes place to an individual or the masses brings new wisdom—and through this wisdom comes enlightenment, and then enlightenment will lead you all to self-realization of the soul.

The body, mind and soul are therefore connected—in order for you to grow and experience whilst you live and resonate with the vibration of energy upon the 'earth-plane'. Realise your soul is not bound or restricted by shape or form, though … otherwise your love and light would not shine through, from, and to me. Similarly, how would you dream, and how would your thoughts float in the ether and touch one another across time, space, and many dimensions?

In addition, if your soul is permanently 'housed or fixed' within the bodily structure, why can't you see it? How have scholars, scientists, and professors throughout time—and across all lands—failed to identify exactly where it is within the body? They cannot. Because they do not witness the truth with physical eyes alone.

Your love, light, and the plumes from the flame of your heart—and indeed your very soul's existence—may only be comprehended by true vision. This comes when you have ascended ... liberated from the cycle of rebirth and death.

So, as stated before in the lesson entitled 'Freedom', appreciate you are already free. Bondage of—and by—the body and mind, is but a notion and false concept! Therefore, let your soul take flight with the self-realization of just who, what, and why we are 'one'. Like a beating heart, I am the essence flowing through your core, and I am your other wing, which will enable you to soar into eternity and bliss forever. Amen.

LESSON 3:

CANCER AND ILLNESS

These words flow through you because they are predestined, and so the text will be simple in its explanation regarding the subject above. I deem this necessary, in order to clarify information—collated over many generations across the globe—and which has unfortunately complicated human thoughts, words, and deeds. For this reason alone, we require simplicity both to and from the individual and the masses.

Therefore, I put a question to all those who wish to identify the truth, what does 'cancer' mean to you? Most people would explain and discuss a source of pain and a disease, which causes anger, hatred, and fear amongst man, woman, child, or animal alike … and the fact there is no preference for age, nationality, colour, or creed.

This is correct, but those with true knowledge of 'self' may also state cancer is powerful, remorseless, and undignified, and is amazing. How and why could anyone or anything describe its context in this way? Well, perhaps a scientist or biologist would. One reason is because of its ability to defy medicine; another is because someone cannot yet eradicate cancer, despite years of research and medical trials within, or by, humanity.

One should realise this 'disease' has been around for many millennia, and way beyond your 'earth years', but what is its point and purpose? Well, for this answer, you need to delve deep into your heart, as if diving into a pool of truth. Cancer is not random in attachment. Neither is it airborne, able to land or inflict pain upon a 'victim' in any haphazard or anomalous way. Indeed, you may also believe that fear of such an event could even play its part.

Remember, please do not be frightened by any man made or other infliction upon the body—which is fleeting—and but a passing moment upon the hands of time. Once you comprehend this, everything will become clearer, with the recognition of who, what, and why you are as you are. That said, I am not blind to the agony the body endures, because I realise, understand, and cherish it.

People with a somewhat doubtful outlook—of this text—may suggest I enjoy these dark shadows, which cling to one's blood vessels, bones or organs, but those who cross over after bodily decay, and recognize their own divinity within themselves, know it is this I 'enjoy' … the celebration and bliss of the liberated soul.

Therefore, appreciate cancer is an illness and a disease, which can spread like wildfire, whose flames burn across acres of forestland with dense smoke without compassion or mercy. Similarly, cancer cells grow and multiply, evading natural defences almost at will. Some people even compare them to a machine, in their 'workman' like demise.

Yet it can rarely be controlled, cajoled, or pushed aside to lessen its effect or condition. So, in your millions, you pray or simply ask, "Why should I go through this heartache?" Alternatively, one may even scream at the top of their voice, "How could my child—or brother, sister, mother, father—ever deserve this?"

Well, do you deserve it, or perhaps … was it ever requested? Are you now confused, saddened, even angry or frustrated by these words transcribed through a 'pen'? Shouts will also ring out, "Requested? Why would a loving God ever allow such a thing?"

First, one must understand I decree nothing at all. You are individual souls, yet we are 'one' light shining brightly with love. For this reason, if an individual develops cancer … family or friends who are physically free of the disease may still become touched by the prevailing anguish from those who suffer with it.

Just as the light from the Sun radiates around the world, so too are the feelings and thoughts of hearts and minds, whether they're negative or positive in design or function. Similarly, the bearer may feel the physical pain; but those in proximity will feel emotionally hurt, too.

Please comprehend, it is essential not to fear the death of the body, for it is a mirage or false curtain which needs to be thrown open and pushed aside for the light to rain in. As love knows no bounds, it can delay, slow down or even cure the overcast shadow on the body.

It is vitally important to remember, it is the soul's own decisions and choices which were undertaken prior to rebirth upon the 'earth-plane' which have a massive influence on the outcome. As bizarre and strange as it may seem, I do not see so-called life or death this way. Again, you simply 'are', for there is only the illusion of separation, which keeps denying you the concept of your own reality.

Many of you will wish to know what defines or causes cancerous growth within the body. Well, these cells or 'triggers' are in all beings, in every animal and human. Millions of you will pass over from simply old age, having had an active life. Others, in contrast—through personal choices—incite stress (mainly self-inflicted), or hereditary DNA links, will also ignite those triggers within. These will occur because we mean them to.

I will now hear angry shouts and cries calling this 'fate or destiny', but it is more appropriate to express this as cause and effect. I waste nothing. Therefore, new lessons are learnt every day for your own personal growth as a soul. Be strong, and in your fortitude—no matter what the result—know I love you beyond all things. There is absolutely nothing which can detract from this truth, fact, and reality.

Remember too, my love for you is unconditional, and therefore I cannot be cast aside by fire, wind, earth, or sea. I am impossible to dilute, fragment and break, for I am constant, both shadow and light. I am the pure and clean, and the dark and poisoned cells within you too, and I am all things in all places.

In addition, I do not make mistakes. Everything has an explanation and a reason, so accept each moment of your earthly existence with freewill and use the choice of what you do in the time you are given.

As stated before, even in illness, there are those who can smile, those who fight for justice and truth, and those who help and encourage others to do the same. They rarely complain, even to another soul—and so become a witness to my truth. In fact, I will carry your burdens, because I am the strength you require through any illness within your life, and I place a protective shield of love and light above, below, and inside and out of you, too.

By your true heart, you can call upon the angels and archangels, the saints, and all of my light hierarchy through me, which are at your full disposal. Please believe with all of your heart the divinity which lies inside you, and in this way, no cancer, illness, shadow or pain of darkness and doubt can ever keep us apart. I love you all. We are one into eternity. Amen.

LESSON 4:

CREATION

When you are sad and your heart feels separate from me, you imagine I am distant in some way, shape, or form. So, I request that you, your family, and your friends—or indeed any living thing within creation—do not feel this way ever again.

You may try to question why these notions of isolation should even enter your mind, but the answer to these issues is, for one reason and one reason only, 'attachment'. Coming to terms with—and accepting—the need to 'let go' is a crucial part of educating your heart and soul, so I will explain more about this shortly.

Remember, while there are those who become aspirants of truth, most people do not seek the genuine purpose of living or being. Therefore, they only see an occasional flash of inspiration and knowledge. However, no matter what level one thinks they've reached, if you live upon the 'earth-plane', there are always lessons to learn.

In addition, whilst the acquisition of the material and wealth exists, such desires will constantly smoulder and burn within the individual and the masses. However, the accumulation of money—or anything else—is not wrong or harmful, unless an attachment to it radiates more brightly than the love you actually are.

Subsequently, it becomes easier to follow a path of bondage and discontentment, because of a misplaced craving and the belief these things will quench a thirst or fill the 'belly', when in reality, it simply occurs from fuelling a negative flame. The aspirant must therefore rise above these issues whenever they can, but do not misconstrue what I now explain.

People often seek me in the same way and somehow need to reattach themselves. As stated earlier, I am not separate from you, and am in front, behind, above, below, and on the outside of you, so how can I be out of reach? After reading or hearing this, you may now think I must surely be 'within' you too, and yes, this is partly true, but in truth I am all of you—your whole being, everything. This becomes much easier to understand when you pause and consider me as 'creation'.

Each night, millions of souls will gaze upon stars, galaxies, and the firmament above them, only to gasp in awe at such beauty and magnificence. Meanwhile, scientists, scholars and academics—throughout the eons of time—all contemplate the 'big bang' and evolution, continually wondering how, why and when it all started. However, if you can appreciate the simple and straightforward statement of 'I am all things', then you must be everything, too.

Once again, do not try to find me in faraway places. Just remember, I am the wind upon your face, the water you drink, and the ground you walk on, too. Hence the universe, which lies beyond your mind's perception, is only a reflection of my love, my body and my being, and hence, what you sense, see, feel, touch, hear, and taste are all one of the same.

So, if you were to continue with this train of thought, you may wonder if you were really 'born' at all, and did you manifest as a soul by some magical potion? The answer is, of course, no. Therefore, as you are light, you have not gone away or come from the light. Your true essence cannot be filtered or watered down because you are whole … and only your own false realization can trick or deny this to you.

With so many attitudes and misunderstandings concerning creation, it is vital that you realise and find out your own beliefs and thoughts about this reality. In this process, you should not abandon any religion or spiritual practice which seeks truth … nor offer me flowers or fruits in gratitude for my love and support, as I do not require such things.

It is far wiser to honour and love the real you and be true to your own divinity. This is the course and path all must learn to take, so do not even believe I attached you to me, as this is a false and misleading 'need', which wells up within you. By loving yourself, you will love the truth inside, and openness, trust, faith, and many other qualities will manifest themselves through, too, and from you. Know that this is true creation in action.

I appreciate many people will read this text and still wonder about evolution and the manifestation of life and energy, matter, and anti-matter, and so on and so forth, but please return to simple thoughts and understanding. For instance, when your tears fall, does the well of your heart run dry? No. Upon death of your body, would you suddenly become closer to me? No, because you are neither separate, divided, near or far from me.

I ask you to have faith in yourself and acknowledge this truth, and then you can truly flourish, becoming a brighter and more vibrant being and soul. In addition, you will grasp who, what, and why you 'are', and this will reveal you can move forward with increasing devotion and deductions in your goal. Only your karmic debt and your life's choices can slow you down, but even these can be swept away by living in, with and through right conduct, as a human being and a real part of the world's society.

We are one, and so there cannot be any dispute or confusion arising over the concept or words of 'what is mine'. Everything 'man-made' is perishable or impermanent, while life existing through love is immortal and everlasting. Do you realise and comprehend this? Indeed, you can make things happen, joyful or otherwise, you only need to believe!

Trust in me, for I am here for you all, and know every heart, mind, and soul. Therefore, please understand there are no secrets you can keep from me (I am I); and you cannot hide, just as you cannot hide from yourself. Try then to be happy and content, and yet strive to achieve and express your inherited gifts, too.

Know the reservoir of my heart is always full, and it flows to, through, and from you. I want you to ride upon it, like a crest of the wave, enjoying the journey to the shore of eternal peace and tranquillity.

Believe me, when I state you have such a special opportunity in this lifetime to step off the rebirth treadmill, so do not even wait one or even 1000 new lifetimes. One must find me by finding yourself. All life is but the size of my fingernail, and yet your love is more powerful and beautiful than you could ever imagine. With this known … light up the path within your heart and complete your very own creation! Amen.

LESSON 5:

SIGNS

Welcome to one and all ... and even though the 'body' may be tired, let your heart be willing to listen, hear, and feel my love. Please understand, throughout time and history, millions of souls have searched day and night for the light. Some climb mountains, believing they become nearer to 'God', while others cross vast seas or sail upon rivers of water and emotion in their attempt to find me. In contrast, there are those who just know the truth, and do not even need to close their eyes in order to sense or 'realise' me.

It is strange that so many of you try to discover who, what, and where I am in these different ways. On occasions, desire can make the 'seeker' believe I resemble buried treasure, and by digging around, they will somehow find the answers to their prayers. Do not mistake me, for I will never belittle or chastise anyone. I urge you all to search with honesty and endeavour, and so this lesson and passage of information are for everyone who requires a helping hand. Alternatively, it can be for a single person and soul who imagines I am hiding from them—like a thief—deep within the night.

So, from the moment you open your eyes from sleep, until darkness descends once more at the end of your day, what signs can be seen? What do you need, pray or dream of? Would you like divine inspiration, and if so, in what 'shape or form' should this arrive? What stone needs to be upturned? Is there a guru or religious figurehead which you must visit to progress?

Like a traffic light, are you waiting for it to turn green, as if pausing for my permission to proceed? In addition, why do you wait for anyone or anything in order to step closer to me? Understand that your journey is not a new road or discovery, but is your existing body, and the path you already walk!

For some, the embodiment you find yourself in may be less—or more—than you think you deserve. However, do not despise or over analyse such things, but embrace your current life or situation. Know that in whatever the circumstances, you are never, ever alone. You are 'me' and I am you ... remember.

Besides, I cannot take 'light' from anyone of you, as this is the permanent core of your soul. Only you can do this—through some self-fulfilling prophecy—to resemble a lamp covered by a blanket, and live, sleep and exist in the shade … when in fact your light, both internal and external, can shine brighter than a billion Suns.

Please try to rise above any negativity that picks and irritates the body and mind, most of which can be deflected and dissipated by sending out thoughts of love and kindness. Simplicity is invariably the key during times where doubt or anguish raise their ugly head. Simple truths will also provide clarity and enable you to power ahead.

From an early age, children will look for—and need direction—and support. Likewise, spiritual education ought to be undertaken with commitment, passion, and endeavour to help you (the aspirant), in achieving your goal of self-realization and eternal bliss.

So, where does one find such things? Who does one seek counsel with? What books must you read? Do you need to visit sacred sites? Well, realise all these are secondary and only steppingstones towards me. If I am everything, then it is your own free will and conscience which dictates otherwise.

Therefore, by opening your heart, you will identify the love you are and can become. But what can you do if you currently think you're lost or confused? Well, should this be the case, please stop this train of thought and do not let your mind trick you at any stage of your life, because the effort you now make is unquantifiable.

Try to imagine your arrival in a strange and unfamiliar city. Everywhere you look, there are buildings, roads, districts, and suburbs that startle, frighten or even intimidate you. Do you fear crossing the road or boundary into the unknown, or do you forge ahead with the challenge and task of discovery you yourself had set?

Appreciate that by turning within, you will realise and sense my help to make your decisions. Then you'll understand that in reality, those street signs and maps all equate to elements in your life, like your job, house, family, relatives, friends, and so forth. Some of these will go hand in hand; while others will appear to move forward and alone, as if they are separate from you.

Often, these roads will be smooth in your life and deemed pleasurable and happy for you. Then, as a new day dawns, and a corner turned, your entire world may seem to be thrown upside down. Each of you will react differently, of course, and yet it is your own re-action to your 'action'— similar to cause and effect—which will affect and weigh heavily upon your emotional and physical health.

Comprehend too, as you age, those days, weeks, months, and years will fly by … though the opposite occurs in your childhood and teenage years, where they appeared to pass slowly. Later, as time becomes more significant —during adulthood or retirement—one will distinctly hope to find the truth and destination, and the real meaning for their life.

So, perhaps all you need to do is to travel up the next street, or one could even believe a sign will illuminate above you, bathed in a heavenly glow. Picture some words upon it right now—in your mind's eye—as it might say, 'ONE WAY!' ... 'AHEAD ONLY!' ... 'FOLLOW THE LIGHT!' ... 'THIS IS TRUE!' ... 'JUST BE POSITIVE!'

One may really wonder where this will actually lead you. Could it direct you through the maze of complexity, the jungle of confusion, and the heartache of joy and pain? Indeed, if you decide to pause and reflect upon your own truth, the sign will simply say in bold letters, 'YOURSELF'. This is because the road, path and current lifetime will only guide you towards the reality of you. The journey travelled is the one you created for yourself, both from now, and from the many incarnations of embodiment!

Please understand, you are living this amazing chance and opportunity, which knocks on the door of your soul. So, follow your heart and do what feels right for you within your life, remembering not to hurt anyone or anything, and be a help to whom or whatever your path encounters. While doing so, please try to weather the peaks and troughs of troubled waters with dignity, for I will lead you to the safety of the shore, because I love you more than you could ever realise or know.

To conclude for today, know deep within your soul lies the peace and tranquillity beyond your wildest dreams. Once you find me, you will discover yourself, and then you will fully understand and comprehend the clearest and most profound sign of all. Amen.

LESSON 6:

HEAVEN AND EARTH

Throughout the world, every second, minute and hour of the day, there is someone, somewhere, whose tears are falling, and religion, faith, sex or age bear no relevance, as their emotions cascade like water over rock.

For me this is constant, and when a soul returns to the 'earth-plane', the 're-born' cry through both shock and apprehension of their new physical presence, and the clearing of the airwaves brings but a subtle relief to the acknowledgment of a new life ahead. Also, upon death and everything in between—be it joy, sadness, elation, pain, loss, gain, infamy, or fame— hearts will ache and sometimes break.

Many will describe their experiences of life on Earth as hell, while others may say they already live in a so-called Heaven, but please try not to label them (or think and believe in these terms), for in reality this is not the case.

Since time immemorial, eyes have gazed towards the stars and light, which seem to shine high in the night sky, and so humankind will contemplate in a two-dimensional manner—with this sense of an above and below—as if they are separate or divided from each other. Nonetheless, if you are all things, then everything is you, a reflection of the truth. Likewise, the magnificence and the beauty of what you call space is contorted by its own word and meaning, as it is not empty, or contained and surrounded by some parameter or boundary.

In contrast, rules, and ethics—which governments around the world set in place for society and the masses—do not bear relevance anywhere else. They exist for your physical embodiment only, and right or wrong (or so you may believe), play no part. Therefore, one could stipulate or state their influence would dictate how a person grows and matures from a child to adulthood. This is marginal, because your character and personality will be tested not only by the environment in which you live, but even more so from the love shown and shared between those who are close to you.

Please understand, even within the vagrant, a beggar or a tramp's heart, light can shine more luminous than a star in 'space', or those who get celebrity status of fame and fortune in the world.

Similarly, regarding resonance and vibration, the planet your physical body lives upon is a brilliant, precious jewel; a fountain of light that continually pours forth opportunity and creation for your life, too. Indeed, it also enables you to grow and identify who, what, and why you truly are.

Every moment gives you the chance to share from your heart, and what you freely give with love transcends far beyond the walls of your home or shelter in which you reside. This is because love is not man-made, but is everlasting and sustaining ... unlike impermanent structures, or a false cage or box in which some of you seem to trap yourselves.

It is as if there is a parallel universe of fear and doubt, when in fact you are all already free ... please remember this! Whilst you exist there on Earth, working, living, and acting out your life's role, at some point you will begin to question your purpose and the length of physical existence. Again, do not fear in these matters, and understand this simple analogy ... life is the car, you are the passenger, and I am the chauffeur.

Therefore, I always sense and know the thoughts and prayers of those who are concerned about their body and soul, and where they think they go when they die. Some will cry because they are frightened of the unknown, as if a blanket of uncertainty covers their light (just as I mentioned earlier), while others rejoice in the feeling they are somehow coming 'home'.

Once again, this can be misconstrued and portrayed with an image of pearly white gates—manned by saints not sinners—and the 'oneness' of me, 'myself' and I as 'God' ... waiting to discriminate between so-called good and evil. Just remember, I am love ... and I love you all. I do not chastise or ration such care and trust to those in favour; but each person attracts and emits positive and negative vibrations and energy, which can appear magical and inspirational at the same time.

The result of which allows every soul free will, with choices and decisions to make both day and night, which can be deemed spontaneous or part of so-called fate. Perhaps it is even karmic balance, and a personal debt required to be repaid. Appreciate the 'time' I give you must be used for love and growth for yourself, and for those around you within society too, as society lives or falls by connections to its core values of peace, good conduct, and righteousness.

What you can view—and I also witness—can resemble a virus spreading out of control, or the opposite, a precise molecular structure like inherent DNA ... organized, defined, and perfect. Love and light are the prime example of this, while hate is the reverse, being random, wild and carefree.

So, where do the Heaven and Earth fall into this equation and process? Did I create these within a certain timescale? Where will your soul go when your body dies? Many seek answers ... but the response and truth lie inside the questions you already ask.

For instance, the Earth is physical in appearance and structure. You walk upon it and so it appears very real to you. In contrast—for millions of people—Heaven is not tangible to the touch, and so they think they cannot see or sense it … and so, like many things, it becomes something outside the truth.

However, if you can comprehend you are living in some sort of ordered time and reality, then the key is to let your heart and mind become free to believe beyond this. Indeed, you are the key to unlock the wisdom inside, and all you need to do is to be still to find me 'within'.

From this, the realization of your 'higher self' will materialize. Once known, you will understand the truth, that multiple dimensions of light and energy—with vibrations of love—enable life to exist beyond your wildest dreams … not separate, above or below, but actually in the same place and time.

Likewise, there is no limit to your divinity or of your experiences. Limitations only occur because your mind tricks you to believe otherwise. Therefore, one can think of Heaven as a mysterious, special place to go to for growth and wisdom of the soul, or it can be sensed right now, precisely where you reside.

In fact, every single hope or dream can manifest, but you must first surrender and stop imagining only 'you' can achieve a desired outcome. Denial of the true power and love within you really means you are denying both yourself and m … so you need to lose the attachment of your own false boundaries. This way, you become stronger and more positive, whilst displaying real attributes and worthiness to be called a human being.

Understand, no matter where you live, or in which country you were born, all are one. Religion should not dissipate this notion. You must realise the foundation and basis of all should be love. So, whether you are a Christian, Muslim, Hindu, Sheik or of any nationality, colour, creed or faith, do not feel or think you are above or below, and more or less worthy than another. The seas of the world have different names, but in reality, they are but one ocean.

Appreciate the Earth and Mother Nature are beautiful beyond comprehension … expressed in truth and love; and appear for your joy to behold. Heaven is but a microcosm and reflection within your own inner search. Surely to deny its existence means that you reject not only me but also your own true self, and one cannot exist without the other.

I will always help you find the truth, and thus you will find me. Remember, I am light, and you are Light … I am love, hence you are love … and I am all things, so all things are you. Therefore, open your heart once more to source the power of your own creation, for Heaven and Earth go hand in hand …. hence, I am with you, always and forever. Amen.

LESSON 7:

HAPPY BIRTHDAY (SAI BABA)

Welcome to all those who will read—or hear—these words flowing through the connection to and from my heart. Right now, many of the devotee's, aspirants, and disciples of love and truth will desire to celebrate this day and night, and may even want to sing, dance, and gather in vast numbers within great halls, or in complete contrast, sit quietly contemplating upon our oneness. In doing so, you wish to honour me with the light, which emanates from inside you, so please realise I 'feel' this far beyond the bodily senses you possess.

Understand too, I recognize your thoughts, hopes and dreams, and know your soul better than you know yourself. Therefore, as you smile and uplift your love to me, I request you should also rejoice for your 'self' too. Remember, all who walk the path of true human values incorporate peace and truth into daily life, and wear the garland of divinity, which can be displayed without ego or pride.

One must comprehend I came to you via this embodiment, many years ago, and this is well documented and spoken about. Please understand though, I have walked the 'earth-plane' several times before, and have been called Saviour, Lord, Saint, and Avatar, amongst many other names. As we are one, it is important for me to do so when required. So, believe weakness will return to strength, and evil will give way to goodness across the nations and continents of the world.

You could say I am happy today, not because of your worship and devotion, but because of what you sense in me as this body of 'man', which is the reflection of your own inner heart. Appreciate that as you celebrate my return upon this annual date, in reality, the celebration is your own.

It is essential you identify and understand this, for rather than celebrating your own birthday—which then reminds you constantly of your own rebirth and the cycle of life and death—you will come to know the truth through me, and thus through yourselves. In addition, across many countries, prayers and good wishes are 'thought' or spoken, both in and from countless hearts and minds. Appreciate these resonate and resound across planes of time, space, and dimension, whilst your negative actions do the opposite, reverberating and sometimes spiralling out of control around the Earth.

I comprehend everything. Yes, the past, present, future, and all life. No one can hide from or deny the light within your hearts and souls from me. What may seem even stranger to you is the denial of one's own divinity, because at some point, every soul—upon their own journey and earthly embodiment—will question and try to understand their existence and purpose. Therefore, you must seek the truth, which lies 'inside' oneself and deep within the religions of this world.

As I have said before, I am not asking anyone to deny—or even accept under any pressure—one's heritage or culture, other than to believe in what resonates in your own heart. So, let this be true with kindness, compassion, and purity.

Of course, if you were to celebrate your life in any other way, we could deem it thoughtless, careless, and even pointless. Should this be the case, how or will your soul then feel? What would your progress and divinity be worth? Therefore, whatever you are sensing right now, do not be worried or perplexed or because...

I am the shoreline and your safe harbour.
I am the firm and smooth ground you walk upon.
I am the air you breathe.
I am the Sun that warms your face.
I am the hope of your change.
I am the faith, which burns away doubt.
I am the tears that melt your heart.
I am the attainable dream of bliss.
I am the goal of liberation,
And I am your true desire.

So, when my physical presence no longer fills your eyes, do not fear this false absence and imaginary space, which is all a mirage. Whereas the truth, as I have stated many times, can only be revealed when the eyes of your body, soul, and mind are one.

As such, I will not fade after these few earthbound years have passed, and the legacy of my current embodiment will forever be etched upon your heart. This is a facet of your own majestic brilliance that shines brighter than the stars you witness within the firmament all around you. And, regarding this day, as many gifts and tokens of your love are laid before my lotus feet, these many thankyou notes and presents show me your true feelings. However, I return these tenfold to mark the commemoration of your own knowingness. Therefore...

I accept your strength and your weaknesses.
I accept your kindness and your devotion.
I accept your pathways, which each one of you takes,
And I accept your love and light, too.

I do not forget any of you. So, understand, while size, colour, creed, and nationality may try to divide you, you are all of one heart and sparks of divinity … fixed upon me since time immemorial. Know that just as I walked among you in the past—and they carry my embodiment about in the present—I will always be all things to you in the future.

Now, with these joyous scenes on a wonderful day, I bear witness to this 'light' precession connecting souls across the globe, so may you find the comfort and peace you each deserve, which is your own birth right. Believe too, as you sing or pray alone, or within a gathering this day, the notes and thoughts will resonate and reflect both pitch and sound, sending your hopes and dreams beyond the physical body.

The hierarchy of light, along with the souls of your family, will shine and shed their tears of love for you all. Each tear will leave a trace of my divinity, which will become a beacon that attracts the same, to expand further than the walls where you live. Know too, this will be perceived 'inside' of you, and by those who have also opened their hearts too.

I will not deny true love, for you are the same, without difference. You cannot diminish by anything other than yourself, and so raise your 'self' to greater heights of your being. Do not restrict your spiritual education and do not feel you are less worthy than anyone or anything else. This way, you will become more than you ever thought you could be.

I empower you to express and follow your own divinity within you. You can 'walk the talk' by believing in yourself, and in turn, you will believe in me. One day, you may even sense angelic forms, which both hover and float with unimaginable grace and beauty. Appreciate they protect and guide you all, so know them in your hearts, if your eyes are yet to see. Their light and love are my gifts, forever peaceful and knowing what is right for you at all times. This present celebrates our union and your perseverance, with your continued faith and trust in yourself and in me, too.

Today, some of you believe my 'birthday' is a reminder that I am physically still with you, but millennium cannot break or ever take away the thread of my gown, which binds and links you all together and my crown of hair will forever remain in both hearts and minds. Indeed, every single soul is like a root, fixed eternally from the tree of life with my love.

Overall, this is but a fleeting day you are celebrating, and yet it is me—I AM I—who bows and kneels at your feet, to celebrate you without end. Finally, remember we are together forever, and we are all 'one'. Amen.

LESSON 8:

CELEBRATION

As you sit and ponder over life, you will soon realise the importance of this day, when people will gather in huge numbers around the world to celebrate the 'birthday' of an Avatar, a joyous occasion indeed. If you can truly see from the heart, then you would become delirious with happiness and peace, as the energy and vibration that flows and vibrates from an individual and the masses will encompass many cities and nations, and the radiance of 'oneness' brings wondrous feelings of being complete—without fear, anxiety or frustration.

This unique event radiates in the same way Lord Jesus gave his sermons, and when Krishna appeared before Arjuna and his army, and upon many more events throughout your so-called history. Please understand though, even in celebration of my love—within these bodily incarnations—try to remember the true meaning of the birthday in question.

In reality, they do not direct specifically these congregations towards me or for my benefit alone, but if they are not, then for whom? Well, the answer is easy, because this is just an annual reminder of your own rebirth into physical embodiment.

Of course, we can also say that such occasions bring together those who are 'close' to you, and this is the positive side of these gatherings as you re-connect and link and establish yourselves as 'one' family without realising it. Then, all must comprehend the love surrounding them, even though it is nothing more than a reflection of the self.

Therefore, millions of souls rise and re-join their hearts to me through my embodiment of Sai Baba, whose earthly presence is 85 today. In bearing witness, what do the eyes portray to the heart … an elderly man, or divinity that reflects and blossoms inside your own soul? Appreciate the question, because there are those who are close to this 'body', but who still cannot sense the sweet fragrance of love's purity, compassion, understanding, and patience.

In the opposite of such a circumstance, one may seem distant, living in faraway lands, but grasp the truth and light from me through Sai's presence inside their heart or mind. Most (human) relationships are like this. For example, two people can sit right next to each other and yet they can be worlds apart; hearts frozen in time, or their feelings for one another become erased by the external behavior … materializing through their thoughts and words and deeds.

The reverse occurs when the divinity within recognizes 'oneness' in all. Remember, distance and time hold no barriers, and are not a prison to true love—here you could think of a mother who imagines her separation from her child. Even in strenuous circumstances, where division seems to have occurred, deep down the connection between them is never lost. On the surface, it may appear to be broken, but the link forever remains.

Justly so, is my union with 'life' on billions of worlds and planets within countless galaxies of time and space, even though all beings and creatures outnumber—by millions of times—the combined grains of sand upon the Earth's deserts and shores. Like dot to dot upon paper, all are 'linked' as one, through so-called good or bad and dark and light.

It is this connection which reveals your joy unto me, and so today's celebrations in India bring smiles, singing, prayers, and thoughts of hope and faith to the forefront of so many hearts. Do not be particularly concerned, though, with the trinkets of such occasions, for even golden chariots (which you think must be worthy enough to carry divinity), will eventually fade to dust.

The true seat of a soul is inside your heart because it cradles and protects your light and the essence of truth. It can magnify your divinity or appear as smoked glass, which obscures the precious flame from view, preventing others to feel and know the real you. Therefore, one must keep the host vessel clean, for like the windows of your home … over time, one may not peer out from the inside. More importantly, the light glowing within will appear dim and often fade from sight, and subsequently anyone who draws near will only fall foul of anger, deceit and hate.

A soul living this way resembles a faulty lighthouse, luring passing vessels onto jagged rocks, submerging another into the waves of emotion unleashed by the torrents of hysteria, lies, jealousy, pride, and ego. Though please do not be dismayed—upon such an auspicious day—and do not worry or fear, because the eyes of truth are forever watching over you all.

Okay, moving on now, as it is an Avatar's birthday, would you like to give a present? And if so, would it be physical, or perhaps an emotional one instead? What do you believe you could give right now? Remember, your pockets do not need to rattle with coin or filled with paper money, because my love is free and unconditional.

It is not vital for you to appear before my embodiment as Swami (Sai Baba) either—where you would have to travel across continents and seas—as I witness your truth through, from, and to love in all manifestations and embodiments. This is because accents, shapes, and sizes are all exterior energy and vibration, and not your true self.

Also, wherever you reside, so do I. By seeking me, you are pursuing your own reality, and realising this will lead you forward. Appreciate, as you grow in body and mind—though not necessarily in line with your age—you will comprehend whom, what, and why you are.

If you can, try to picture the scene as banners wave gently upon the breeze, and petals fall before the elegance of divine feet, which—for those who are close by—appear to be almost floating, effortlessly, above the floor.

The sound of 'voice' will soon reverberate into song, as man, woman, girl and boy congregate far and wide ... if only to glimpse our manifested 'purity and love'. Many hands clasp tightly together, held close to their hearts in thanks for their prayers being answered, while some are outstretched, willing the love and light of 'my' embodiment to be touched. A sensation and feeling of another sort of reconnection may yet be made, and of course this is a privilege, but for whom?

Well, remember your light is my light, and therefore I recognize this in your desire to be close, and so I will draw even closer to you through your trust, faith, perseverance, and love. These are the true gifts you can bestow upon me if you so wish, and in and through these you receive me too, for taking one-step towards me. I will have taken so many more to you.

Now then, as you contemplate what has been 'transcribed' from within; overcome any uncertainty from all circumstances around you. Celebrate your divinity and mine as one. Rejoice in the communion and communication that cannot fade or disappear ... one which many doubt, but never fear.

As you come to me by finding yourself, your tears may often fall. They will be tears of joy and bliss, soothing and comforting to you like a long-forgotten kiss. Please understand then, a celebration can be so precious, providing an opportunity for all to partake throughout time immemorial ... and this becomes another true reminder of our everlasting friendship and 'oneness' into eternity. Amen.

LESSON 9:

MERRY-GO-ROUND

I bear witness to your mind and heart, and therefore know everything you think and say and do. As such, I observe the tension and concerns which have enveloped so many of you at this time of year regarding Christmas preparations, work, and money … not to mention one's family and health issues. There seems to be little time, not only for yourselves but also for me and us.

Remember, I am 'love', so I will never become desensitized to whom you are, but through discernment you could all recognize the unimportant things, and those parts of your life which are no longer required. In fact, it is down to each one of you to establish and confirm in your own minds the reasons you act the way you do. This, together with the words you speak, will connect with other hearts in more ways than you can ever imagine, influencing the energy and the vibration element of love and light to become brighter, or dense and thick like sticky molasses.

It is precisely at these times when one's priorities should be second nature to you. Realise too, that your health, family, occupation, and home are all factors which affect the wider community and society in which you serve. This is significant, because if souls around you shine more brightly, the canopy of light will encapsulate and protect you, too. Therefore, how much effort do you need to make? And what about the attention to details to be made by the few and/or the many?

Well, in attempting to answer these questions, please remember that even though we are all 'one', people still imagine they are separate from me within and around their life. So, let me remind you of some words and images revealed once before, in the hope you can become more dignified and understandable as a human being, continuing to grow and display true characteristics required to rise above negativity and false desire.

Picture this; a family who are planning a holiday together, and they would like to embark on a journey, perhaps somewhere warm and far away from home. By dissecting these 'plans', what does one find? Well, much time and energy—and often with blind faith—are all being used to steer this wish to fruition.

One immediately places trust in those travel arrangements and to arrive at their chosen destination on time. Likewise, they hope the desired accommodation will be safe and clean, that the Sun will shine, and there is enough food to eat. To arrange these few and simple actions takes so much time and frequently consumes one's thoughts each day.

Compared to this, many souls around the world spend very few moments turning 'within,' or even try to feel the love that I AM while they sleep, talk or work. It is as if their inner light and I are 'pushed' to one side, almost forgotten by the blur of life's merry-go-round.

Therefore, what does this lifetime require the individual to do? How should you conduct yourself? Are there inherent and unseen forces preventing you from stepping off this cycle, or rebirth and death? Please understand, even though this revolving door is spinning slowly, most souls somehow cannot reach for the exit. So, you must realise it is 'you' who are the hub, the mechanism and force both positive and negative ... and your being and traits and actions and karma are all spokes which attach you to the wheel of life.

Your knowledge of such will resemble a repair kit, like a sticky plaster over the puncture of forgetfulness. My love will glue and prevent any further escape of the truth from within you. Surely, this will bind you and enable you to ride along your path and destiny more smoothly. You also need to remember your burdens on this journey are mine too ... so just ask me, and I will carry them for you, if you can truly trust me to do so.

Ironically, when you experience so-called 'good' times, how often do you forget me? Do you ever sense me in your joy, happiness, and elation? I state this because more often than not, I will only hear the 'call' when disaster strikes, or if there is pain of body or heart which pierces through the light. This resembles lightning and thunder shattering the peace of the day or night, in a desire to command my attention, pleading for me to intervene and erase darkness, fear, and dissatisfaction.

Please appreciate, if one's expectations do not materialize in the way you hope, it is me who becomes lost, cast aside in fury, anger and doubt. Even though this happens, I will never abandon, deny, or place you at the rear of any pretend queue. Each of you is part of me, so I cannot forget one element of life, no matter where you live.

You must therefore return to simplicity and stop denying yourself. The door is unlocked, and you have not lost the key. You are the key. Through your own efforts, you can approach the door of truth, and open it with righteousness, dignity, honour, knowledge, and wisdom to gain your bliss through self-realization.

When the door is ajar, the shaft of light will erase the shadow, forcing it to disappear behind you. Then, and only then, will you be a witness to the truth, which both captivates and frees you from the false burdens and anguish you have made. Appreciate one should not fear what lies before you in this lifetime, but see the path as an opportunity beyond your dreams. Remember, if you cannot agree with this, then you cannot accept yourself or me.

Therefore, as the Sun rises and the dark night descends at the end of your day, your routine can remain the same, or by keeping guard against your own loss of morals, and with your duties, service and help towards others, the possibilities are endless. Indeed, you can be the rainbow which lifts another's heart, or the water to quench the thirst of another. You can nourish the unfortunate, and can provide warmth, shelter, comfort, and care in innumerable ways to your fellow man.

In these, I can work through you, for I am at your disposal. You must remember all of life receives what they need, more often than what they think—or believe—they want. So be thankful, because your requirements can be the complete opposite of someone else's, and therefore the connections of love and light and truth may be complex in their execution—indeed complexity within your own thought process and its eventuality—but not so in mine.

In addition, everything is for love and love is for all, and so the time humanity places upon these is irrelevant and unjustified. Now, as the year ends, try to imagine what you think and feel you can become. The sky is not the 'limit' as your true vision may appear restricted, so use your heart to picture the correct desire and truth, which is inbuilt into your body, soul, and mind.

Comprehend that complex DNA cannot even compare, as the matrix of love is beyond explanation or justification, so you only need to understand it is you, me, and everything eternal, because it shines since time immemorial. Believe and acknowledge this, and make your dreams, hopes, and wishes come true! Amen.

LESSON 10:

SORRY

Mmm, and so it comes to pass, and while I can describe the events of the day with words, they are simply not enough, are they? And, even more so, when what we say becomes elevated into shouts and screams ... whipped up by anger and frustration, all because they contain the same doubt and fear. These fly from the tongue, emitted like fireballs, knives, daggers, and swords, which only blind or pierce another's heart.

Also, one's feelings are too raw, while shame, anguish and uncertainty surround you with a concoction of emotions that poisons your being ... and as this currently reigns in your home, it attempts to replace the love for each other.

The Christmas tree may be lit, and yet the shine and glow are fading. In fact, inside, you feel and look dark, for 'love' seems buried deep down inside oneself, and those thoughts, like an avalanche of rocks, cascade from the mind to suffocate your hearts. They appear divided, becoming separated, pulled apart, and miss the spark of light lying behind a false curtain of pain.

Appreciate, if emotions can make the body curl up and hide, then the heart—which contains the love that is you and I—can also shrivel and appear to fade like dust ... and die. Remember, hurtful words are far worse than wounds to the impermanent body, the latter bringing injuries which can heal relatively quickly, but when the heart is battered and bruised, it takes more than a sticky plaster or bandage to mend it.

Throughout time immemorial, and since the embodiment of humankind, the division between man and woman and man to man has ensued through lack of knowledge, wisdom, compassion, and understanding. Indeed, what a person or nation sees as negative or wrong is only the reflection of one's 'self', so there is no cure or magic potion to be offered to the other, because the sickness or 'dis-ease' lies within the initiator of the action, the deed, or even the very thought alone.

Therefore, what can you say or do when your tears have fallen like water over a rock? What solution, glue, or medicine and cure do you think you each country, or even the world, needs? You may believe you want or desire status quo, balance, and equilibrium, when what you really need is peace, compassion, and above all, forgiveness. But how can this happen when another will not speak? How can you repair what you cannot touch? How can you look into another's soul when your eyes will not even meet?

The answers do not lie in any earthly place. Conflict, disputes and divisions cannot be solved with presents and gifts. Everything which is free must flow from the heart—and your love—so the spark of divinity within you can rise like the phoenix from the ashes. You will emerge from the cocoon of sleep, and bloom from a chrysalis into a new butterfly, becoming stronger and soar higher than you ever thought imaginable.

I can help you ... for you will appreciate and know I am always the answer. And by focusing upon the truth and love inside, you will find 'time' provides the opportunity to mend, grow, and cope with those troubled periods of your life. The emphasis should be to change from materialistic concerns to those of the family, of your wife's, husbands, partners, relatives, and friends ... after all, you are one community, one society, one race and there is only one true religion ... love.

Therefore, do not worry over what is 'yours or mine' or fear any loss of attachment. Do not become agitated by inconvenience and even sorrow, for these are the traits you can actually control. You must be strong-hearted over an often-weakened mind, which makes you believe you cannot survive or flourish in those situations of your life you yourself have made.

Remember too, because I am you and you are me, you contain the power and strength to overcome diversity and pain. The choice is whether to acknowledge this, and to comprehend we are 'one'. So, as I see those false painful flashes from broken hearts rising through the dimensions of time and space, know that each second and every minute, hour, day, month and year, I sense them too.

No matter who, what, or where you are, I promise you nothing is in vain. You will all flourish, and through faith in love and light, you will discover the answers you seek within yourself. Please understand too, the word 'sorry' can be whispered or even shouted from the rooftops to those you love, but if their hearts are closed, it will remain unheard.

However, do not force or be in a rush, to prise open a heart which lies behind a hardened shell, for sorrow leads it to be fragile, liable to further damage, and the one who is attempting to do just that may not fix the bearer. You only need to be true, and in so being, become a human with values of righteousness, honesty, truth, devotion and love, and leave the rest to me.

Strive to achieve and do the right thing—in all forms of relationships— and this will guide you towards the path of self-realization and bliss. Hate and anger should play no part in any aspect of body, mind, or soul, so view all circumstances or situations as a test from, through, and to yourself. Hence, you can evolve, or you can become withdrawn, hiding, or even diminishing one's own light.

Realise the opportunity to remove oneself from the cycle of rebirth and death is always there, for you all possess the ability, but you need to recognize this. Can you imagine—when your body fades—feeling sorry for not being the person and soul you could have become? If one is truly remorseful for all things said and thought or done, I will know this within your whole being, because love is always a witness to truth and sincerity.

Understand this lesson you read or hear is not to coerce and force or make you fear any eventuality, but to help you be aware and become all you are meant to be. I therefore urge everyone who is going through—what you call —disturbance or pain this day … do not hate yourself (or others), and do not regret. Things happen; you cannot turn the clock back. You must move forward quietly, carefully, patiently and tentatively, so listen to your heart at all times.

Also, do not allow the ego to raise its ugly head, and try to conquer trickery and false promises before they find rest, take root, or spread. Cultivate the field of love instead, with the seeds of and from your heart, in the knowledge they will not wither and die, because I nourish them with my light and fountain of truth.

Understand you shall reap this new harvest you sow to sustain you into eternal life and the bliss of peace and love. It is here and here alone where you do not need to think, feel, or share any words or emotions of sadness and despair. In fact, 'sorry' may be the hardest word to say—when said in truth—upon the 'earth-plane', but within my heart it does not exist, and is never, ever, said at all. Amen.

LESSON 11:

HOME

I sincerely hope that you not only think about the words on these pages but also sense them in your heart too, because they aim to keep your attention focused and true of the important things in your life.

Now, as Christmas approaches, one's thoughts and feelings undoubtedly turn to family and friends both near and dear at this special time of the year. In addition, regarding your festivities, one cannot but wonder about 'home', and those moments with those who matter most.

Why do you feel this way? Is it tradition, or perhaps your faith? Is one's home where the heart is? Of course, it is natural for someone to conclude this refers to your earthbound dwelling, whether made of wood, tin, brick or stone. This is likely to contain even the bare minimum of comfort, be it straw for a pillow, cardboard for a bed, pieces of rubbish for a fire, or even the opposite, having luxuries like shelves full of food, a feather mattress, electricity and gas, or shiny televisions and gadgets which attempt to entertain your mind.

Therefore, no matter where and when one thinks of home, memories of sustenance and well-being will come to the fore, which pulls on heartstrings, and makes you wish you were there. And, if you are where you think you ought to be, perhaps someone special, such as a friend, brother, sister, father, mother, lover, partner, husband or wife, are not.

In this scenario, it is easy to imagine a separation exists between each other, be this through time and space, or even by the veil and curtain which you call death. However, try to remember, above all things, they are actually as close or as distant as you think or believe them to be.

Realise the heart is not just the functioning organ of the body; it is everything, because your heart is mine too, and love unites every soul. Therefore, the connection—when your true desire takes hold—can be as weak or as strong as you make it. Indeed, they say absence makes the heart grow fonder, and if you believe this, take comfort knowing that 'time' may seem so important, but in the grander scheme of things, bears little relevance at all.

Please appreciate, love cannot dissipate and fade like water upon the sand, evaporating in the sun, and therefore the so-called 'separation', even for one minute—or for what transpires to be your whole life—will eventually reveal the truth. You will realise the differences between what is real with the misconceptions the impermanent world tries to impose on you. So, do not gaze towards an empty chair. Instead, hear their voice, see the look in their eyes and smile upon their face. Sense the touch of their hand too in the knowledge they cannot ever be erased, for they are deep inside your heart.

In fact, you may think they have disappeared or somehow drift far away, trying to find a way back to you, but do not feel hurt, sad or grieve, because you must understand, they are not, and never will be lost! I am with every single one of you. I know where each soul resides every second, minute, hour, day, week, month, and year, and for all eternity.

I comprehend so many hearts that ache. They are often torn in two, but just remember, I am like glue … who always returns and binds you all together. I love you, so how can this not be so? I realise one's pain can drive deeper than any blade upon the body, or how words can cut more quickly, and take a lifetime to heal. However, if one can help, share, and speak with truth and love, and another's heart is open and receptive, then it, too, can be given the time and strength to mend.

Know I will be the plaster which is 'cast' towards you by this reality, to repair broken hearts and protect you from the infectious mind and the brittleness of a weakened faith … especially when trials and tribulations seem too much to bear. One day, all souls will appreciate they are on a journey, and each one is different. That said, the destination is the same, and, through self-realization of your own divine essence, you will come to realise your genuine home of bliss and peace.

Within me, your dreams come true. Every day is magical … with love eternally beating from and through and to your heart, and you will recognize this in all its glory. Therefore, by opening the door to your own heart, the Christmas you could only ever imagine becomes reality. Inside is a welcome you will never forget, with cheers and tears of the happy kind, and smiles without fear.

Each room is decorated with pearls of wisdom, and they are all illuminated by both starlight and the 'son'. There is no hate or pain, only truth and fun. There is no empty chair, just two hearts which beat as one. Family, friends and pets, and teachers and guides, all pass through and by, to greet and meet you.

Surely by now, you must accept this gift of love is from no 'secret' Santa, as the glory of you is not meant to be hidden away, or pushed aside to pretend it's for another day. No, for every moment is an opportunity to share and sprinkle the glitter of your own divinity.

Sometimes this will rest where you think it should. On other occasions, the words you speak, the gestures you make, and your love will shine and travel to life in the most unlikely of places, throughout time, space, and every dimension. You may not bear witness or understand these results, but that is not important, because every act flowing from your heart transcends and elevates precisely where and when I intended it to. Do not worry or concern yourself over the 'result' of these beautiful actions, for I know the where, what and the how.

So then, with the festivities only a few days away, please reflect upon a new beginning and the rebirth of truth, which has been nurtured deep 'within' yourself. Love has grown inside with all the ingredients installed from my heart to yours … faith, righteousness, non-violence and so much more.

Our connection cannot be severed, and our divinity is my crowning glory for all to witness and partake. Therefore, through infancy, one's youth, in middle or even old age, there is the opportunity to shine through your love, which I have presented and pre-sent to you with all we are—and I am.

By opening your heart, all who draw close will recognize the light, and share in something precious to behold, for all eternity. This is my timeless gift to one and all. Amen.

LESSON 12:

HUNGER AND THIRST

Welcome to all hearts and souls. In a few days, I will remind you of a special day, but even now, after over 2000 years have passed since Lord Jesus' birth, both mystery and intrigue still shroud this miraculous event. Some say the date is inaccurate, others insist it never took place, and then there are those who wholeheartedly know and sense the truth, which links us all together as 'one'.

Indeed, throughout time, many people search for reasons to follow different faiths, as each display numerous figureheads and statues, along with ancient written text all bearing the testimony to a religion and/or way of life and living. Therefore, what drives one person to be like this, and for another to deny all aspects and existence of a 'God'? And, who is more worthy of my love and light … is it only the aspirant, the devotee … a disciple or follower of truth? In addition, is the non-believer going to head towards darkness and decay, through denial, especially of self?

Please understand, I do not judge such elements of who is right and who is wrong, because the principles and guidelines of human beings are the same. If someone is an atheist, may they still be a 'good' person and soul. To be a Christian, Muslim or to follow—and live—by any religious doctrine or faith of truth is to be true in thought, word, and deed, too.

Remember, as each day of your life begins, I bear witness to everything you strive to complete, with those tasks and duties you—or others—set. During these activities, the body craves and desires food and water, so partake in these as and when necessary, not before or after. (In this modern age with countless time constraints, moments to enjoy and savour them seem to have all but disappeared). Please realise, you will suffer physically, in minute and infinite ways, through such denial or through neglect—and worst of all—through starvation.

So, this Christmas time, what will you consume? Will you overeat and drink, become bloated or even ill? By taking time to enjoy what you consume, this will cause improved health. So, as I stated before, please try to achieve this by partaking in the following proportions, ½ of food, ¼ of water and ¼ empty stomach … this way, one should feel as light (in weight), both before and after. Does this expose a current lack of self-control, and do you now wish to change your way of life?

Well, herein lies a bigger challenge, for do hunger and thirst solely belong to desperate trials and tribulations of the body alone? No, not if you can bring your soul into the equation. In these busy times I mentioned earlier—whether through neglect or abuse—do you often sweep such thoughts under the carpet, trying to hide them from view, wishing they were out of one's sight, mind, and heart?

This is the worst practice of self-neglect there can ever be, but why? Well, any man, woman or child who is starving or severely dehydrated, will say the body (which is acting through the mind), will take precedent over all other concerns, insisting it comes first. Everything else is secondary and of less importance.

Do not misunderstand what I mean here, though, because without a healthy body, you cannot function properly, and it becomes more difficult to attain, meet, and transcend beyond your earthly goals. Through a lack of understanding, many people try to find the easy life to live, but down what route does this lead? Is it a road to nowhere?

Now think about your soul's true goal of self-realization. Does it not hunger for greater sustenance too? Would having a purpose actually sustain you? What text could quench your thirst for truth? What knowledge would satisfy the inner craving so often ignored or denied by circumstances of time, effort, or even ridicule from others?

Know you are who you are, and by always accepting yourself first, other souls will surely follow suit. You can be who you were born to be, and experience 'life' in any way, shape and/or form, as long as it does not harm you or any other form of life.

Therefore, where are these golden nuggets of love, light, and truth? Are they stored upon supermarket shelves, or cast beyond your cost and reach? No, for I am constant, available 24/7, not divided or separated by any religion, faith, colour, creed, or caste. I am no 7/11 convenience store either—unavailable through the night or only within certain places, towns, or cities.

My love is free, deep inside you as your divinity. Like a flame and a beacon, it illuminates infinitely beyond the boundaries of your home or wherever else you live. Therefore, appreciate that by withdrawing from the impermanent world, even for a short while into stillness and peace, you will become energized and motivated in your well-being. Yes, the well of your heart is indeed the place where you can quench the thirst within your soul. In addition, strength and power will follow through the nourishment of love and truth deep inside you.

Jesus once said, "I am the bread of life. Whoever comes to me will never go hungry, and whoever believes in me, will never go thirsty". So, please understand, even if you read no sacred texts such as the Bible, the Koran (Quran) or the Vedas (to name but a few), the wisdom that belongs to you and you alone, lies in the stillness of your heart. Like your favourite sweet, chocolate or candy, after you taste the sweetness of your own being, you will desire and wish to share it too.

There is a key difference here. While food and water are the sustenance and fuel of the body, the soul will never become satisfied with bite-sized chunks of nectar. For once you dip your toes, you will long to dive headfirst into your own divine essence. This can cause unintentional shock waves to your family, friends, or acquaintances, as they may view and treat you differently, but only by living your own truth, with courage and conviction (and most importantly, with love for each other), can these then be turned into softer ripples, and soothing energy.

On occasions, the acceptance of another will happen quickly, while other times may seem like a marathon, a long road and journey ahead of you. Please do not overly worry and become frustrated though, or believe you will need to make such an incredible effort that it might as well be beyond the stars or Mars. Remember, within you 'I am', and I am everything, the true source and energy to help you in your work, rest, and play, and I have a sense of humour too!

But is there anything holding you back? If not, what treats are you going to uncover and reveal to your higher self? Well, the greatest gift you can give to your own—or another 'body', is both food and water. Meanwhile, the most desired present of the soul is for sustenance from the pool of love, which does not dissipate, freeze, and never prevents you from partaking. It will always fulfil, guide, teach, and forever want to satisfy your eternal hunger and thirst 'beyond' the body and mind. Go now, in peace and with blessings, for I wish you all a happy Christmas. Amen.

LESSON 13:

COMMUNITY

Be still, for you are all welcome in the presence of the Lord. Therefore, please try to understand, even though it's difficult to overcome squabbles and indiscretions of friends, family, neighbours or even strangers who cross your path in daily life—it is important that you do. If the individual cannot rise above such things, their communities in which they live are unlikely to either.

Appreciate my love and light connects every one of you, and therefore societies will not function properly if people, streets, and communities become divided by hurtful thoughts, hearts, and minds. It only takes one element to cause friction and dysfunction, which subsequently disrupts peace and harmony. You could relate this to those Christmas lights so many of you have now packed away, as one faulty bulb will ensure the string of lights fades and disappears.

Before you ask me, yes, you're right, this is not always so easy to do, because of the way someone acts or by others being influenced by what they said. I am not requesting you all to become or live like a saint, but perhaps one can try not to be a sinner. Do not be mistaken by this word of 'old', for if no one made a so-called mistake, I guarantee you there would be no souls residing upon the level of vibration and energy you do today.

What I suggest is always constant, for when the flames of anger rise within, just stop, and rest the mind. Realise you can control the mind more easily than you think—though it requires you to be more cognizant of it, so you can bend and shape your thoughts with truth and in love.

When the flames of hatred, desire, or even frustration flicker, try to reason with why you are thinking this way. What is the cause behind it? Why do you feel the way you do at the precise moment? Asking yourself forces the mind to track back upon itself, causing a loss of focus. Hence, the fire is dampened because the thought process has been altered, and it is as simple as that.

In the beginning, you may struggle with this notion, but as your life experiences ebb and flow, you come to know and grow with truth inside your heart and soul. I explained before—long ago through this connection and pen—so much can change when you link hands and hearts with your neighbour. There are many occasions in Earth's history, and indeed throughout all time, that show and clarify my point.

Therefore, through times of so-called trouble, a kind gesture or even a smile can reignite the spark of truth within. Selfless acts always bring out the best of—and a change—in people, and the respective outcome can be karmic or otherwise. Simply showing someone that you care can transform and lift the energy in any place or time.

Remember, being present is not a requirement of truth, because communication and love are the key to unlock darkened rooms inside a home of light. By opening the door through softly spoken words, no voice will become raised. Angry flames cannot rise, and they dissipate and burn themselves out.

You do not always have to be right within a situation of disagreement or conflict to assist with a calming voice. In addition, with prayer and divine thoughts, the power—which exists inside you—can manifest across time and space. These two dimensions cannot withhold or diminish the love which connects a true desire to help another soul, being, animal, or indeed all life itself. Know it is the belief, passion and the integrity behind these thoughts and actions which I sense and realise in truth.

Every one of you has a rightful part to play, so it is essential to know at this stage of life that the 'walk on' role makes the 'scene' complete. Without all the characters and different personalities, the beginning, middle and end of any film or play upon the 'earth-plane'—or you may imagine some other scenario or situation—cannot reach its conclusion. Would you want to watch a movie with only one actor? Likewise, would you ever eat a cake without half of its ingredients?

The world needs to understand every person, community and country are equal, so how can any life be more precious in the west or the east? Are those who live north of the equator more important than those in the south? In reality, you all need each other in far greater ways than you imagine. This is not just in commerce, trading or of financial ways and means, but also in real terms of creating peace and harmony. This will happen only through trust and friendship, and not in trying to impose the will of one over another.

People can start by supporting another person or even the community, by spreading one's wings to other villages, towns or cities. Sharing knowledge and experience, while providing help in truthful ways, also shows real kindness and love. Comprehend that humanity displays the evidence and traits of hope and compassion when natural, so-called 'disasters' take place, be it tsunamis, earthquakes, floods or fires.

This, in turn, begs the question of why the 'blind' eye is often turned during famines and war. One nation or continent should not think or feel with the attitude of 'it is nothing to do with me' or believe this type of statement can suffice. Who knows when the conflict reaches different or nearer shores? Understand, there is always cause and effect, for one cannot exist without the other.

Likewise, man and nature must live more in harmony. Harnessing the assets and beautiful energy from the planet you live upon in more positive ways would be a start. The human race also needs to comprehend all life is sacred, because each animal, insect and creature contains my love and truth. The only difference between these and yourselves is the fact the kingdom of nature does not know it—yet. They are not 'God' conscious or aware, man is.

Therefore, you could class the understanding of such as a privilege … and a necessity to fulfil the soul's goal of self-realization and bliss. This permanence is not in different time zones or across the hidden depths of space, but is the love deep inside you, which all require and should experience. It cannot be crushed, broken, burnt, or dissolved, and is immeasurable and without end.

If just one person strives to change his character and life while sharing from the fountain within, my love and light will pour from the well of their heart. Many will come to drink the goodness drawn forth and will quench a thirst so parched. Your divinity and essence will shine throughout the world, and then you can all become the true beacons of joy and hope everlasting. Amen.

LESSON 14:

ECHOES

Welcome. As you sit, there will be those on the 'earth-plane' who still wonder over what you know as 'time'. In fact, so many of you consider the year is drawing to a close, and therefore cast your minds over the passing days, weeks, and months.

People will also reflect upon the choices they had made, decisions that were taken, and words or actions they should have said or done—or not … as the case may be. Then, as each of your seconds and minutes tick away around the imaginary clock of your hearts, thoughts and feelings often materialize inside the mind. These, in turn, cause you to contemplate your relationships with those around you, and the true values of your existence and purpose and divinity within.

Now, across the world, statements like, "Where has the time gone" … "I can't believe it's nearly New Year" and "It doesn't seem five minutes since last Christmas!" remind you that time waits for no man. This is the link to make you think. So, please appreciate your past, present, and future are all entwined as chains of energy and vibration, which carry your heart and soul through karma, experience and life.

In reality, you can do much more than live in the moment, and this is to love the moment itself. By loving what you do and speak, your being positively shines like a beacon for others to bear witness far beyond the body. This is because the light of the heart—through action, thought, and word—resonates upon many levels, and is, in fact, sensed in very similar ways to sound.

Imagine a row of bells—in a variety of shapes and sizes—for as they chime and ring in different waves of pitch and tone, each reverberates and echoes. Your life experiences resemble this, and your future will usually reflect those actions of past deeds from your own karma, too. From this there is no escape, and easier to understand when some say it is by some pre-ordained fate for each and all to contemplate.

Now visualise you are aboard an old submarine. You cannot see where you are (and what is outside the vessel) with physical eyes, and therefore sound is emitted and returned to locate your position. This is an echo, an imprint, a reminder of what and where you are, and so you should naturally comprehend you are all 'echoes' of me, too. Each light and soul can never be lost or alone, even when you think you are.

Understand that in the depths of despair or pain, I sense and know everything you experience and feel. In your joy, happiness, and elation, the petals of your heart open and bloom, while the rays of the sun (and Son), both shine and beam down to make you radiate in truth and peace. In all times and places, 'I am I', and because you are me and I am you—unlike the echoes of sound upon the 'earth-plane'—you cannot disappear, you are permanent and everlasting.

That said, your essence and divinity could actually fade and diminish, not from the radar of love and light, but from each of your own—and others— memories. This is the reason behind many incarnations, and why your own self-realization is so important to change yourself right now.

Therefore, your exterior needs to reflect and echo what is within you and your true heart. When this happens, your life and all around you becomes one in peace and harmony. Conflict, anxiety, fear, and anguish are all by-products of anger, desire, and lack of control over your own thoughts and senses. Controlling the lower 'self' re-ignites the power, passion, and determination of your higher 'self'. No person can do this for another, as each one of you must make your own choice and decision. Night and day, different time zones, minutes, hours, weeks, months, or years, bear little or no relevance here.

Thus, by being still, you will hear me, for your heartbeat and rhythm blends with mine as one. In the silence, the understanding will come and reveal itself, if you believe it to be so. Do not search for answers in transient, exterior, and impermanent things, for they will only deceive you with a false thirst for passing pleasures, and these drain your resources both material and emotional.

I do not imply you should live a pauper's life, hide away in a remote cave, or even deny yourself comforts of the body ... only that you should try to be content, especially when your senses attempt to deceive and trick you. Worse still, if they actively lead you to cause pain upon another person, animal, being, or soul.

You may well ask for help when indecision comes. Well, I am your conscience, intuition, and your 'gut' feeling telling you whether something is right or wrong. Try not to over complicate these matters, as simplicity is the key. It is important the heart controls the mind and not vice versa, because the mind is full of trickery, attempting to placate your inner voice, all the while suggesting why's and wherefores to satisfy its own agenda.

In its effort to reason, one is encouraged to fear ... and embrace negativity and doubt, so truth is often quelled or denied. Simply put, the heart knows of what and when love grows, whereas the mind is a tool; a vital cog, but still requires self-control and constant checking. You can achieve this by listening to your thoughts and establishing whether they are 'sensory' or heart induced. You can then move forward on the right path, knowing it is for your higher good.

However, by subduing your current reality, you will often think or say aloud, "I wish I hadn't done that!", but do not despair or dwell on this. Rise above negativity in the fact you now recognize such things. This will strengthen your resolve, and grow even brighter, able to guide others in their own quest and search, too.

Realise, unlike a ripple upon calm waters, love's action transmutes way beyond the pebble thrown into the pool of life, so understand there are no boundaries which cannot be broken or removed. Differences of colour, creed or religion are on the surface, and humankind needs to dig deep to discover the truest connection of all.

Sometimes, a lot of effort is required in doing so, like digging through frosty ground. However, when the truth is sought with conviction and faith, you will break through to find softer earth and hearts. There, deeper within, the soil—and soul—is warm, and the cold cannot penetrate any further. Likewise, even those with hardened exteriors have 'love' waiting to be both discovered and shared.

Appreciate love can—and will—melt away any last remnants of distrust and confusion. You only need to be ready and willing to let yourself become more open to the reality. Remember, too, I have passed the written word down through earth's history in many tongues, sacred texts, and signs. By becoming more aware of love's echoes throughout time, space, and all creation—and which resonates inside all hearts—you will understand it is part of the greatest wisdom you can know. Amen.

LESSON 15:

ARE YOU AWAKE?

Welcome to our connection once more. You now realise this stillness brings you the ability to recollect, and much needed peace. This is your time away from the pushing and shoving of your daily tasks, which can bury your heart and mind inside a darkened cloud of confusion. Only within can you elevate beyond such density, to bask in love and light, and become refreshed, rejuvenated, and revitalized far greater than a so-called holiday of a lifetime could ever do.

Please understand, if someone's thoughts are constantly drawn to the exterior world of the material, we can describe life as living in slumber. One may walk, talk, and use their senses, but the heart lies unconscious, resembling a coma or deep trance. The body—a garment of clothes wrapped around your soul—will usually arise from sleep, to work and toil throughout the day, and the mind continually 'thinks' Most people call this living; but in fact, it is just existing.

Therefore, it is quite clear and apparent, that to embark upon your own journey of truth—no matter what colour, creed, country of residence or even the religion or faith you follow—your divinity needs to be re-awakened … removing the belief in the so-called reality of the physical world. In essence, all you see, hear, touch, taste, and smell are reflections of the joy and the eternal wonderment residing inside you. Indeed, all senses there become magnified—way beyond the comprehension and normal thought process of most human beings—because we cannot find everlasting bliss and peace in the dense realm in which you currently live.

Realise, if one lives outside of their true self, you remain unaware of the truth, which reflects, resounds, and radiates as love from within. So, do you need something of a divine nature to occur in order for you to sit up and take notice? What alarm clock or interruption can assist you to experience and know the light, and understand what is right?

Well, what you require is not man made, for this would be impermanent and fade away. Only the resonance and vibration of love can motivate, lead, carry, rescue, console, heal, nurture, forgive, and remember 'itself' as one. Love does not force or cajole another to see a particular viewpoint or reason to exist, but guides and encourages the connection to one's heart to beat to another tune and frequency, away from doubt, darkness, and false pain.

I sincerely hope these words will be like a fresh spark, re-igniting the fire in you, a universal source of power and energy which jump starts your heart into action—your new and eternal 're-action'. In fact, as you become cognizant of your realization and goal and purpose, it may seem as if you are awakening from an operation. At first, your mind can be fuzzy, unfocused, your vision unclear, and then, in what appears to be a short moment of time, your true sight will return.

Appreciate the pathway and scene ahead, for a new dawn is upon you. You can look towards the rising Sun (and Son), which warms your face and heart, and you will smile and radiate with delight, because your illusion and delusions will disappear like a rain cloud. Your soul, now becoming enlightened and 'lightened', shall beam with joy, while the colours of the rainbow shine and spiral both near and far.

All this and more are within your grasp, as if inches from your fingertips, and all you need to do is to ask for, desire, and realize this with all your heart. In your actions, know I do not judge any of you, or grant or deny requests or wishes. Understand, it is the soul who can determine far more … than the mind likes to make you think and believe.

Therefore, you must free it from negative thoughts and traits. Do not give way to the "cannot, will not, or shall not" attitude. All this does is to restrict me from working with and through you and attempts to weaken our connection. It shall not break, but your freewill may cloud the issue, and even try to deny whom, what and why you are … so just remember, we are 'one' and this can never be diminished or erased!

In addition, whatever your current circumstances or situation, it is yourself who is more powerful than you could imagine. Of course, there will be tests, trials, and tribulations, though should you confront them with endeavour, fortitude, perseverance, compassion, and understanding, these make you even stronger. Know you can channel this into amazing gifts to help yourself and others, too.

Understand that if you become 'hurt', criticized, or condemned by another, please forgive, and forget. Likewise, do not dwell or succumb to ego when you assist or help too. (As I have said before, overlook the good that you do). Many people and souls do courageous and brave deeds each day. They are unrecognized faces whose hearts swell with love pumping through their veins, and do not need medals or certificates to display their acts of kindness. Instead, they bear witness to the truth within themselves.

Comprehend their knowledge and experience, which gives them wisdom. This is shared through hands and voices, freely and openly. I am not saying I need you to be a hero, but state it is down to you if you want to change even a fragment of your daily life. Therefore, ask yourself right now if you are living for 'you', or whether you could have been a better father, mother, son or daughter, relative or friend in the last hour, day, month or year. Or do you want to be?

Once again, choices have been and always will be your own. All I am saying is the opportunities are there for you all, every minute of each day, to express the true love you surely are. Remember, I will forever try to encourage, guide, and protect you in all of your desires, and more significantly, your needs of the physical, mental, spiritual, and ethereal realms.

Well then, can you rise to the challenges which lie ahead? Remember, I am calling you, loving you and waiting for you to do just this. Or, on the other hand, will you still slumber—and rest—attempting to resist your life's many tasks and tests? If so, when will you awake? Amen.

LESSON 16:

ICEBERG

You felt the pull upon your heart, David, and know when to put pen to paper once more. Know that I have laid the seeds of these thoughts, together with a desire to fuel the flame of wisdom inside you. In fact, I placed several clues to what this lesson is about, both within your conscious and unconscious mind.

One such sign came over the internet, a picture of a massive iceberg slamming into the ice shelf—breaking off another—which captivated your curiosity and imagination. Another clue was the old newspaper article you read concerning the Titanic, and those who had 'crossed over' after the ship's collision with the ice. Then, only yesterday, you made a sandwich for your lunch, containing 'iceberg' lettuce!

I supplanted subliminal messages so you would focus and understand these lessons are not random or haphazard in any way, shape, or form. Indeed, each possesses their own purpose, position, and a time to be heard or read by the individual, a small group, or by the masses.

So, let us begin today by covering simple well-known facts ... that an iceberg is mostly made of water, and almost 7/8ths of its structure is below the surface of the sea. You do not need to understand its composite molecules and the finite details of its appearance, as the picture portrayed inside your heart and mind bears a greater relevance. Therefore, the larger of its mass is below and kept hidden ... and like a mirror image, so are many people's feelings and emotions. This means the innermost sanctuary of your love is nearly always out of view.

I am not talking about wearing hearts on sleeves, but wish for all to consider their true nature, personality and makeup, the reality of what is 'you'. In addition, one could say the traits and character most reveal are but a fraction of what you truly comprise. Unless you attempt to look deeper within yourselves, then the mystery and the magnificence of your true being will remain unseen ... for while each individual display only a portion of their 'self', the remains are submerged in doubt, confusion, and anxiety. These underlying elements emulate a rough uncut diamond base, which needs cleaning, polishing, and refining.

In addition, an iceberg seems to move at an incredibly slow pace. We can compare the sheer scale of some to small islands which float along in the sea, and yet often appear static, like immovable mountains. Some of you bear the same resemblance. On the exterior, you can be larger than life, firm and headstrong, while others live as floating rocks, easily swayed by the currents of pressure and the winds of change.

I am not saying one is better or weaker than another. Contrarily, this is to make you realise how you view yourself, and not what people perceive or think they know you to be. No matter what size or shape of your physicality, it is a garment and cloth for the soul, but nonetheless, one which you should protect, cherish, and love. Do not be confused with its attachment, but understand its importance, as your body enables you to live and be you upon the world … and the current journey of your spiritual education and development.

Comprehend this too, that the ice, with its rough and broken edges; resembles and emulates those negative traits, which often protrude towards your fellow 'man'. However, they will become worn smooth by love and through good conduct, righteousness, peace, and truth … so your current vessel—or yet another 'body' of water—will no longer become broken, to drown and disappear in a flood of tears.

The iceberg will melt over time then, and its shape will change and diminish as the energy and currents of both sea and air alter its appearance from above and below. Likewise, over the years, your own attitudes and attributes will effectively reduce the shadow beneath and behind you. It is nothing more than the cause and effect of your own karma, but the divinity containing knowledge and wisdom from within your heart will replace it. Your soul can then flourish, blossom, and shine like a rainbow over time and space.

As I am light and love … I am everything you can ever need, want and desire—and you are too—for I am I, as I have stated many times before. Believe, feel, and know this to be true, for you are the sum of all things. So, you must now delve deeper into the stillness inside you to find those answers you seek.

Travel further into silence and leave your mind behind, for in peace you will know yourself—and me—clearer than before. Please appreciate, your experiences will all be different, and yet the fact remains, each of you will comprehend more than you ever thought or dreamt was possible or imaginable. This is not like a mini submarine, which shines a light, scanning the blackness and depths below the iceberg. This is because you are the torch of truth, and able to shine more than a thousand, or even a billion Suns.

Realise when you become focused, you will soon illuminate all before you, and others may recognize your own majestic brilliance through character and personality and one's deeds. Those enriched by truth will stand out and become visible, like an iceberg above the sea line—riding upon the waves of emotion and life—and then, if you were to ask yourself what you actually want to achieve, you would know, because you can fulfil your true potential.

In addition, an iceberg's age can be many millennia; therefore, its layers deep within its core can bear witness to creation. It may hold the experiences of numerous harsh winters and countless hot summers, and while some eras of its lifespan reflect only youth—just like souls—some are of great age. These help to bring the knowledge and wisdom which lie inside all, but when the hardened heart becomes melted by love, all truth is revealed.

Therefore, over time, all of your bodies will succumb to erosion, and resemble an iceberg, which eventually melts, dissolves, and appears to break up and disappear. And, even though the body shall diminish, subside, or even fade from view, your essence and being has only changed in appearance once more, becoming one with the sea of life, light, and me. Indeed, you may believe you were separate, as if floating away, but in reality, we are together, as the wave can never divide from the ocean of my love, and so forever … 'I am I' you will stay. Amen.

LESSON 17:

RESURRECTION

This is an apt title for a Friday, indeed this 'Good Friday'. So, let go of your mind, and do not let it impart new thoughts, concerns, or any form of anxiety over you at this time. In fact, draw down, deep within yourself, and acknowledge the connection, which can never be erased between you and me ... for I am I, we are all one, forever and a day.

Please understand, there are people, souls and beings who set aside a space in their hearts, not only to contemplate upon such things today but also debate the Easter 'period' itself. For many, each day will roll into the next, the hands of a clock constantly turning, while others find their faith, trust and hope renewed, reborn, and you could even say—resurrected.

Comprehend this does not mean I favour one religion or deem any land or country to be greater—or more purposeful—than another. Those thoughts are within 'man's' consciousness and brain but bear no relevance to a heart of love and truth. No matter what colour, creed, nationality, or even whether you are male or female in bodily garment, all may use these words of guidance and sustenance freely and equally.

Appreciate too, as you go about your daily tasks, time is becoming more precious, because each family home across the globe can house new whirlwinds of pressure, stress, and confusion. This leads to friction, unhappiness, and uncertainty between all members of society, so please use this moment to pause and reflect, and to re-evaluate your reasons for being and living.

In fact, the desires of the impermanent world need to be reined in, and not expanded beyond one's control. I do not state you cannot be comfortable in your life, for all should be, but reiterate, there is enough of 'everything' for every man, woman, and child upon the Earth.

Remember, each person and soul should realise that by continually striving to earn money—to buy more 'things'—will only mean more work. It is self-perpetuating and can be destructive as the exterior tries to subdue the interior of you. Shadows of doubt and confusion can then attempt to block out the light, which leads you God-ward (inward) ... where all your true needs are met.

Okay then, so having mentioned 'resurrection', comprehend this day will always be remembered when Jesus 'died'. (Remember, to believe in this is your own decision). Indeed, while he cried out, "Why hast thou forsaken me?" … I suffered too, as do all mothers and fathers who feel pain when their own child is hurting. Please appreciate, you are never alone, separate or ever divided from me. I am with you constantly, through your sadness and failings, and within your joy and triumphs.

Comprehend I am but a thought away. So, my help, my love and my embrace are there for you. I shall arrive in a smile, in your laughter, or by a helping hand to lift you up. I am with you in the sunrise as the light shines upon your face, or within the breeze and wind which cools your skin. I will be the water that quenches your thirst too, therefore I am with you always, in all ways. All you have to do is to trust and ask me.

For some, I remain a mystery, an enigma, or even a fictitious God. Indeed, in countless different languages and spoken tongue, there are hearts who cannot currently 'see,' for false fear and illusion temporarily blinded them. One day, though, all will see clearly with the eyes of the body, mind, and soul in unison—just as they should be. They will know me in all walks of life and by every heart because truth will prevail, sending 'light' to pierce the darkness and rise through doubt and despair.

Know that Jesus rose from the tomb of death to reveal peace, bliss, and self-realization. This is your goal, to remove the cloak and veil of death and fear and release yourself from the treadmill of rebirth. You can achieve this, but you must make your choice, now you realise your will is free.

Understand too, humanity is the conduit who utilizes the energy and vibrations between the Earth and sky. These are not separate, as they are always in contact with each other. In addition, because all things distribute and share positive and negative energy, how each individual person lives— and uses what is both 'within' and 'out'—has a marked effect upon them and their surroundings, too.

This power spontaneously rises from the Earth through the force of water, air, fire, or even the land, which cracks, bursts, or erupts. Fear, anxiety, anger, and frustration in human thoughts cause these in catastrophic ways. But I am still there, throughout moments of panic, terror, desperation, sadness, and loneliness, as well as those so-called good times in your life.

Therefore, I request, from the flames of fire burning brightly inside you, to know the truth. Like a candle shining within a darkened room, I am seen in all directions, so you do not need to ask where I am, as I am all of you. In another simple analogy, consider me as both a spoonful of sugar and a glass of water. If they were mixed, you could not see the sugar, so does this mean it does not exist? I am the ocean and the wave, which merges constantly, remember.

Right now, put down the burden of all of your cares. I promise you, I will pick up the crosses to bear myself, so put your trust in me—and in yourself —to move forward into the light, with the shadows of doubt falling further behind you each day.

Symbolically, may the crown of thorns prick your mental consciousness, bursting the balloon of any inflated ego to tarnish the soul's brightness. Let the blood from Christ's limbs flow through your own veins and bring the light of the 'Son' into your hearts. And his body, which bore the sins of— and for—the world, becomes a reminder that I will always forgive and love you. It is for you all … who you need to love and forgive each other.

So too, may the robe wrapped around the Lord be known as the blanket of truth and protection. … and I have placed this around you all, yes, for every one of you. Therefore, even in your darkest hour, feel its warmth, comfort, strength, and compassion in the knowledge it will constantly flow and envelop you, because it is only a thought away. I am I, and so I am you and you are me … the Father, the Son, and the Holy Ghost.

There is so much more for you all to learn, as we have barely scratched the surface, but just like the phoenix rising from the ashes, this very minute, hour, and day can be the new you, a new beginning of your life. Understand the power of the physical body can never compare with the essence and energy of the immeasurable truth within you. Through the resurrection of your own reality, you can nourish and cherish and believe it, and it will truly fulfil your life. Amen.

LESSON 18:

RE-UNION

To all who open their hearts, minds, and souls … welcome, welcome, welcome! Now then, imagine you are sitting in a garden. The sun is glowing, and as a breeze flows through the branches of the trees, their leaves weave and dance upon my breath, which seems to call and make you aware of my presence.

Please understand, I wish to lift thy heart, elevating your love to new heights for you to experience and share both peace and bliss. And, even though the title above implies a re-connection—which can create false symbolism inside the mind—in truth … what we write today confirms and brings recognition to the hearts of many.

For millions of people across the world right now, in particular those with a Christian faith—as well as those devotees of Sai Baba—these last few days bring emotions to the surface. However, even despair and anguish can lead to the acknowledgement of truth, and an elation of amazement and realization. During such times, people wonder how a complex array of thoughts and feelings manifest and influence one's heart, by not only shedding tears of fear and sadness, but wonderful joy, too.

Realise too, through eras of old and these so-called 'modern' years, each faith can inspire one and the many. For instance, the Easter period renews thoughts over the resurrection of Christ—which was a victory over death of the body—and the miracle of being 'one' with me. Likewise, with Sai, the Avatar of your current age, who departed his physical body on Easter Sunday morning was not by chance, but as a reminder to everyone of this auspicious time.

Remember, you are not a body with a soul, but you are a soul who wears the body like an overcoat or vessel, which enables experience and emotions to materialize as an expression of me. You could call this a union, a partnership, or a blessing, but only when the physical is discarded, does the important re-union takes place.

Some find this controversial, particularly when a soul undertakes a short sojourn—soul-journey—into the impermanent world, such as a new-born baby or young child. With this notion, do not be disturbed, confused, or cry out with anger or frustration, because you are all divine … and therefore, made your own karmic choices prior to embodiment.

Life is a lesson for the individual and their next of kin, as well as connections further afield, too … like twigs at the end of a large branch on a tree. All are connected in some way, shape, or form. Therefore, cause and effect exist in the relationship between man and all life.

At the time of one's passing, especially those who reach old age, the exterior 'you' becomes weak and brittle through its experience and reduction of energy within the body. Even more so, for those who take on the negativity and the ills of the world, which help to ease the burdens of pain, uncertainty, and fear from humanity. Remember, when the body is spent— resembling a coat with no buttons and holes in the pockets—it cannot insulate or give protection to the internal organs anymore. Like being in a photographer's darkroom, it develops a negative … exposed to more ills than it can bear.

Therefore, I manifest and live amongst you as great teachers, Avatars, and supreme figures of 'Godhead'. Through them, you come to realise the truth. Their brilliance and luminescence could be felt—and seen for miles—such is the power of their love. You should also appreciate that each of you can shine brighter, internally, and externally, right now and every passing day. (These choices, though, are always yours to make).

Throughout history, if people did not witness and experience these miracles of light, the world itself might be so overcome by darkness, hate and greed, you would think it impossible to emerge and live anew. But having done so enables you to bear witness to reality, and I reveal the true image not only for the soul, but to guide many toward their goal, too.

In addition, it does not matter where you live because everyone can grow to understand this through different faiths. This is because they all lead to the religion of love, though their interpretations can dilute, abuse, and confuse, influencing the 'monkey' mind with illusion and confusion. Here, one must appreciate it is not love, which creates anger, conflict or war.

So, where does this currently leave us? Well, because you are reading or listening to this book, you have already taken much more than baby steps. You are beyond infancy, and like a student, you must decide whether to continue in the school of life, through the re-education of your heart and mind and soul. You comprehend the truth, but 'remembering' it disciplines, transforms, and purifies from within.

Picture yourself peeling an orange. Why does one do this? Surely, you can digest and partake of it whole, can't you? You could, but you do this to reveal the true desire of your palate. Indeed, the sun grows the seed, while the water of life nourished and helped it to mature, and just like the fruit and juice, your light is also the essence, your purpose and goal.

You do not hanker for the orange skin, because you long for the nectar inside. Similarly, when you are ready—on a soul level—you peel away the outer layer (the body), which has hidden the true value and beauty it contains. Resembling a mirror image, I can compare those who desperately need to quench their thirst to the desire to unify and merge into me. Do not be confused, for you are already part of me—as stated many times before—but it is you, as a body and soul, who believes you have become detached from me.

Understand then, when your overcoat has been cast aside, I reveal your divinity in all its glory and splendour ... while many friends and family over many generations will have the opportunity to witness and greet you from the false curtain of deceit. Then, while some who loved you on the 'earth-plane' grieve and despair, others (within lighter elements of vibration, experience, and knowledge), know your spark has burst into spirals of light —both beautiful and magical—into happiness, bliss, and peace.

It is important to remember, you cannot purposely remove this yourself, as there are inbuilt safety mechanisms which usually prevent you from self-harming, unless of course ... illness of body or mind dissipates the action of truth. In these cases, many lessons are learned ... both on a soul level, and for the family or friends who believe it left them behind.

Through self-realization, you do not need to peel the orange. By turning 'within' to the stillness, you will find me and feel my love, sustained without the fake glitter and imaginary sparkle so readily available in the impermanent world around you.

Therefore, do not be sad here, and never fear when I am near. All life is but a click of your fingers. One assumes your experience of 'time' is long, when in fact it is but a whisper upon the wind or can seem like fragments of the imagination. This is why your soul could experience many generations of re-birth and karma.

Finally, I would like you to imagine yourself as the only adult and person at a fairground. Would you embark upon a child's ride? Is there a false desire to go around in circles? Is this the moment to come off this pretend playful merry-go-round? Are you now ready to board the express train in the true tunnel of love? No ticket is required ... remember?

KEEP ON TRACK … with SAI BABA

Time to then experience, a journey straight and true,
Stuck onto the tracks, with my love, it's just like glue.
No safety belts or fear, when I hold you oh so dear,
Those tickets not required, being burdened by your tears.

So much pain and anguish, but now you're free at last,
Peace and bliss, our memories … but they come and go so fast.
I had looked at all your life, what you said and you had done,
In truth your love eternal, has more than just begun.

Remember my words reflect upon the future and the past,
As you pass beside the body, some stand and stare aghast.
In visions and in dreams, I will remind you of the truth,
My body was a vessel to be used for living proof.

I love you my dear Swami, please remember that is all,
And yes, received your message … of your Darshan, my one true call.
To continue and to strive, to live through and in the heart,
For we remain as one, forever from the 'start'.

So, mourn if you now must, but only for a while,
As the stone was rolled away, for eternally wide smiles.
My cloth it was pure white … often orange, and next time green,
Deep within your heart, you will know exactly what I mean.

Yes, your life it was a message, and you tried to say it all,
To come unto your bosom, we waited for your call.
Both the rich and so did poor, came from nations far and wide,
For your omnipotence and omnipresence, as none of us could hide.

You may think you're far away, but you're always near and dear,
It is time to stop the crying and the shedding of those tears.
For I am always there, as you sit and when you weep,
My hands they hold your heart, and you are safe within my keep.

Okay I will go, to live in truth part of your play,
Yes, be kind tomorrow, and for you SAI every day.
A need of who I am, and what was born to be,
Still walking amongst us all … beyond eternity.

Amen/Om Sai Ram.

Remember!! Remember the day ... Sung by Ajnish Rai.

LESSON 19:

CLOUDS

As I am all things, including your heart and soul, I sense and know your thoughts, hopes, wishes, and dreams. Therefore, 'love and light' is the fabric of existence, and hence, no separation or division can ever exist. I will constantly reiterate and explain this to you, like a record or 'iPod' on repeat play, until it becomes etched inside your mind.

However, because the mind is fickle and can be feeble and weak, you must remain strong in order to deny the false desires and fears it brings. Effect follows the cause, so clearly one's thoughts and feelings resemble darkened clouds, which temporarily obscure the Sun (and Son), from your vision.

Throughout your life, similar clouds also appear as manifestations of your worries and anxieties, both in the tasks of your daily lives and in those of friends, family, society, and even nation upon nation. It is quite apparent that each individual can affect whatever 'clouds' emerge, because they can easily be dissipated by love, kindness, faith and hope … or they can mushroom into ferocious dark storms with thunder cracking and lightening flashing. All are reflections of the emotions within you, which mirror the exterior (the without), and vice versa.

So, every day the Sun shall rise, no matter where you live or lay your head at night. It is constant—just like my love for you. This is a physical comparison, and the understanding comes from inside you, because when you withdraw into one's 'self'—into the deep stillness of your heart—it is easier to comprehend the truth and beauty from our connection and everlasting light.

All can choose whether to stay away from the illumination of truth—and live in shadow—which keeps your divine essence and conscience under lock and key; like a self-imposed prison cell. Every opportunity to feel the warm rays on your face, and to uplift your 'spirits' and well-being … is gone.

Remember, you have the right and the wherewithal to push open the door to your heart. The pretence that you need to break free from something is the illusion and mirage, leading to doom and gloom and fear. Therefore, when you pause and reflect upon your concerns, I urge you to imagine them as simple 'clouds'. Through the belief and trust you have in yourself and me, they will move away to reveal the Sun once more.

In your thoughts, I will be the wind blowing them through your mind's confusion, to leave you with a clearer, brighter new canvass for you to draw upon, both symbolically and physically. You can picture how your day, week, month, year, and your life will change right in front of you. Love knows no bounds, and so there is nothing at all humankind cannot achieve, if it is in truth.

So, right now, before you … see your life as a blank page and draw a new image from—and through—your heart. What colours will you use? What textures and shapes can you create from the pallet of love, peace and harmony? Remember, what you produce from within can inspire others too, because your passion, vibrancy and eagerness will captivate their imaginations.

Do not let those old shadows creep and stretch from the corners of the mind, which will hide the way forward and disguise the smoother path ahead of you. Understand I am the pen, pencil, paint, paper, and the canvass, and therefore I ask you to use me by thought and word and deed. I am always here for you—and will help you always—however; it is important to realise that spiritual growth comes through knowledge and subsequent wisdom, which provides you with what you need, rather than what you think you want.

One should know I do not pick or choose what you can or cannot attain, because divine help occurs in the hearts and hands—through circumstances and connections of love and truth—which then materialize your requirements as a soul and a human being.

Understand, once you finish the picture, it can be framed. This will signify its completion and become recognized as a symbol of love's power … complete and displaying truth in all its glory. Please do not envisage your own image/picture, a scene, or even one's desire as more important than any other, for all life is sacred and beautiful. Appreciate too, a frame can be made of rough sawn wood, or glittering gold … yet that can still become tarnished and dull. I explain these things, not to chastise or belittle anyone's conviction, but to highlight the choices and decisions you make and what these create.

Now then, when you wake in the morning, I dearly wish you to see beyond the differences of opinion, character, shape, size, caste, and creed. Change your view of the many who currently believe the world is separate or divided, whether by culture, spoken word, the clothes people wear, or even the colour of one's hair. Each nation or continent is unique and develops in its own way, and yet for all this, your hearts are the same, for they pump the blood, energy and love which sustain you all.

While you are reflecting upon these words, please know an experience or event appearing as a cloud in your life is not necessarily bad. Your so-called darkened times can bring new beginnings, new strength, and new growth in the body and soul. Indeed, even though the mind can temporarily cloud your judgment, these tests, trials, and tribulations can still be overcome.

For instance, imagine the heat of a desert; would cloud in the sky not provide instant relief to those seeking shade or shelter? Of those which rain, do they not shed water for the seeds and crops to grow? Therefore, every cloud has a silver lining. You just need to seek with all your heart, and you will find it. You will gain strength from these lessons, and become more positive in your outlook, to elevate above such clouds and enable your being to bask forever in the glory, love, and supreme bliss of you, me, and all things.

For those who are starting to bloom through their endeavours, please witness the rays of light shining through the clouds upon a sunny day, and know everlasting, they will beckon, entice, and lead you. These are my beams—some call them 'God' beams—piercing shafts of love, light, and hope, into and for all eternity. Amen.

LESSON 20:

RELATIONSHIPS

When you become still, you can truly feel the connection to me and all things. Some may describe this 'stillness' as being in slow motion within your heart and mind, while others imagine they are frozen in the 'moment', inside immense love.

In addition, by bringing calm upon the exterior, you will sense the same inside the interior you. Now, sitting quietly, birdsong can be heard from a distance, and yet its notes of rhythmical sound somehow connect straight to your soul. Well, know I am the peace, the noise, the vibration, the energy, the light, and everything your senses can imagine, and so much more.

Please appreciate, although I mention the word connection—a few moments ago—you and I and all life is greater than this. We are beyond being in harmony together, and more than relations too, as we are all one, but so many people seek the answers to the how and why and exact nature of our relationship?

Before we can go more in-depth on this, think about and understand the link, and those bonds with your friends, family, and fellow human beings, as well as the animal kingdom, Mother-Earth, space, the universe and so on.

By believing yourself to be an individual, you may wonder, "Where do I fit in? Why am I here? What is my purpose, and how can I possibly be important in the grand scheme of things?" Please understand, asking these types of questions only takes away your own focus, which attempts to separate yourself away from who, what, and why you 'are'. It also shows you are unsure, uncertain, perplexed, concerned, worried, frustrated, and anxious, which are all lower forms of energy that divide and cause confusion and illusion. For all this, a spark lies deep within the aspirant and seeker ... a light which is brighter than the Sun.

So, when you search for the truth and the real answer—to the reason and purpose of your role upon the stage of life—you will find it is actually you who are the 'real' star. It is being yourself, forming relationships with all those whom you meet both near and far ... whether this is within the realms of consciousness and ether, or from the audience itself.

Think right now of a film, a play or a theatre production, something which touched your heart and emotions. Perhaps it was a birth, a death, a song, an actor's tear, a beautiful dance ... or a magical scene of splendour like a brilliant full moon, a rainbow—or even rain? All these can have a profound effect to inspire and motivate and bring smiles and laughter to your heart.

These form memories, a relationship with your mind, and they become linked to both heart and soul. Going deeper than this is your past lives, the cycles of rebirth and death, which all formed a link through karmic balance and imbalance. What is so important to understand and realise is our 'oneness' (I am I), can never be broken, but the link to this rebirth cycle needs to be. Know you can progress beyond the physical 'plane' into a permanent bliss of love and light.

However, as your energy resides upon the planet at this present time, one of the most fundamental aspects of your spiritual growth and education is self-realization. One cannot achieve this by fear, anger, and deceit, or by succumbing to sensory pleasures, which are only trinkets and trivialities.

One may think, "Where do I start? How can I develop or become a kinder, better person?" Well, you might believe yourself to be individual, but this is only true in so much you are a fragment, a spark of the divine light. Therefore, you must first comprehend the relationship with each other, your surroundings, and to me, too. If you are a mother, father, husband, wife, partner, brother, sister, or friend—and in whatever capacity of life—you should try to seek, live and 'be' in truth.

Remember, I bear witness to all, and so many relationships create anger, hurt, depression, and separation, a disconnection from truth and hearts. Tears flow, as if grieving for love, which resembles a beautiful vase or vessel containing light, constantly being chipped, and one day, it will crack, fall, and perhaps … fade away.

Someone recently asked you if you thought their marriage could continue, and another said they had made their vows in front of God, and so feared upsetting or offending 'him/her'. Nothing should be taken lightly, especially where children are involved. Appreciate that for karmic balance, earthbound connections—if they have been fulfilled—may indeed come to an end. I do not—and never will—cast blame upon one or another, as I love you all, unconditionally.

Comprehend at all times though, to be selfless, not selfish. Be thoughtful and not thoughtless. Be kind and not blind to another's emotions or heart. Everyone deserves to be happy—and can be—but problems occur when you imagine someone is not being how you want them to be. One's life will yearn to control everything and everyone, which soon becomes second nature. This is wrong, as you are all free to be 'you', and the best person you can be.

Do not imprison yourself through attachment. Of course, I do not refer to marriage here, but in the belief your existence depends upon another, because it does not. Attachments of any kind lead to fear and anguish, and keep false desires, like a thirst which can never be quenched.

Try to understand love is the glue, the key, the religion, the faith, and is the relationship and connection above everything, while unconditional love remains the power and light which transforms the darkness of shadows and doubt into the hope of a new dawn and a beginning for all life.

Therefore, right now, whether it's day or night, just ask yourself the following questions. How important is the relationship with your 'Self' ... your inner 'you' which is I? And what efforts will you make to fulfil your soul and goal? When you can understand your true self and know that love is within and around you—and inside everything—relationships on all physical levels can only improve.

When you see your friends, family, neighbours, community, society, and every race, religion, country, and living being as one, then nothing can frighten or detract you from me. You will never be cajoled, ridiculed, persuaded, forced, or made to feel captive by any false imprisonment ever again.

You and I have always had the special relationship that was, is, and forever shall be. Birth and death can never separate or diminish our light, which is infinite. The world and universe and all time and space and each plane and level of dimension are related. Indeed, we are all one 'relation' within the ship of my heart, sailing upon the ocean of my love. Amen.

LESSON 21:

THE GARDEN

This new day finally allows some peace and calmness, a familiarity you once enjoyed long ago. It seems bizarre why those earthly pressures, stresses, and commitments take precedent over your own true well-being, though please remember; I am not criticizing, but observe the current reality in the way most of you live.

By resting within the stillness of the garden, it becomes a peaceful haven for reflection and contemplation, which will soon refresh and sustain you, too. Now, as limbs of the trees sway gently back and forth—from the breeze of my breath—some leaves float, then fall and land precisely where they are supposed to be. In a similar fashion, many hearts spin upon the highs and lows of their own making, until one day, they find rest, far away from the negative forces and actions which push and pull both thought and mind.

The Sun is shining now, bathing you with warm rays, which you, the Earth, and much more depend. A passing cloud may temporarily cast a veil —like those that obscure the truth—but please know, I will blow a kiss to anyone who cannot lift this shroud from their eyes, for my love and breath can remove any obscurity which blights the true vision of your heart, soul, and eyes as 'one'. Remember, all three need to be in unison, so they may bear witness to the reality of creation.

Birdsong now flows through your mind. I sing for you all, as soft lullabies long to resonate inside your hearts. Insects fly too, while the swifts and swallows swoop and glide effortlessly high above the treetops. The wind catches their flight, and they almost hover, letting you glimpse their forked tails and elegant wings.

The flowers bend and swirl, as if dancing to a merry tune—for this is my melody, my inspiration, and the rhythm of life itself. Several roses dress the border, and even though from the same variety, they appear to be different colours. In spiritual terms, these resemble the many cultures and shades of your earthly 'skin', and yet the fragrance is identical, just like the love and the divine essence you all are.

Appreciate the importance of wholeness and unity, and for this to be recognized and encouraged to replace disparity and separation of your minds, creeds, and colours of humankind. Many acts of both the individual and society imply the latter, when instead a simple smile or act of generosity can bring you all much closer together.

In fact, when you link hands with your neighbour and friends and family, nothing is impossible for humanity to achieve. In difficult economic times, and the forever-increasing pace of your lifestyles; this will become even more apparent each day.

Please hear me, because if any of you are reading this 'lesson' in your garden, stop to pause and reflect upon the life that envelops you. Perhaps you can see a majestic butterfly gracefully floating from here and there, as if without a care. (If you do not see one, try to visualise one instead).

From the exterior, you will not envisage or sense its power or strength, but in your heart, comprehend the speed of its wings, which beat and turn. Now in slow motion, and almost at a standstill, the ripples of sound and vibration radiate and pulsate, creating its own sublime and beautiful aura of love and light, which blend with its surroundings. This field of energy resembles a magnet placed under a piece of paper with scattered iron filings.

So, as you sit within the stillness, try to do the same, and blend with such peace and harmony. Understand, when you remove yourself from this to engage in the activities of the outer senses, you will change. Your being alters because the aura and energy of love and vibration can dissipate and scatter into irregular patterns of hate, jealousy, desire, anger, and frustration.

I mention these simple facts in order to remind you that every waking hour can be used for the good of others—as well as yourself—or they can be misused and wasted. It does not matter whether you are working, resting, or playing, because your thoughts, actions, and deeds forever resonate and spiral in all directions. Your time is the one thing you can use with 'choice', but you have no control over its past.

These are your decisions; and yours alone, for I am not your gatekeeper, but through every breath, I am willing you to do and be the best you can become. I do not judge your mistakes, and I will not forget or leave a single one of you to live eternally in shadow.

It is through these written words—and many others from across the continents of the globe—which can help and assist, but you must only accept what feels right when it resonates inside you. This sensation is clear and precise, demonstrating you are ready for it, too.

Please realise the most important source of stillness will never deny or refuse you entry, as your own divinity cannot—and will not—push you away. I shall never disown you; make you feel inadequate, lonely, or sad either, for I love you all.

I know you better than your family and friends and even yourself. I understand your hopes, dreams, wishes, and desires, as well as your so-called failings and frustrations. Therefore, let go of the past, and any regrets or feelings of guilt, because today, right this minute, can be your new start and a beginning for your spiritual growth and education.

No one should ever say you are below or behind another's knowledge or wisdom. Even a saint or scholar, angels or archangels can achieve new or great things, and yet in love, light and the truth, medals or honour are not required or sought after. Rewards are irrelevant, other than having an inbuilt wish, which seems to require my grace.

Remember, a smile or helping hand—genuinely given to another—is worth more than the millionaire who unwillingly donates money to charity. I am not saying these gifts are not welcome to those who are without, but the energy of love radiating from an open, peaceful heart is more precious than trinkets, diamonds, or gold. In fact, the real jewels which adorn the crown of my heart are your souls, and your tears hang in suspension around me; falling when we 'connect' within. They glisten and shine, and their magnificence and brilliance are infinite, as they radiate more than a billion Suns.

So, remember me by remembering 'us' as one, for the peace you need, seek and truly desire is not in faraway forests or mountains, but inside the core of your heart. Then, through your own self-realization comes the understanding that both you and I—the Indweller—reside in this deep recess as 'one' together, in harmony, friendship, bliss, love and light. Appreciate too, the Sun, which shines down upon you and warms your face, is the grace I give you all each day … now and forevermore. Amen.

LESSON 22:

CONFECTIONARY

Welcome and good day, or should I say, 'God' day to you all. Now, as you sit still and withdraw within, you notice our connection and oneness. Where you are bears no relevance to me, and it makes no difference whether you are sitting, standing, running, climbing, or if you are in the air, under water, upon land or even in 'Space', because I sense and comprehend everything about you.

Barriers do not exit. No amount of distance or time can ever separate your love from mine. Even your emotions cannot deny or take the essence of your divinity away from me, for we are whole and 'one', as I will continually reiterate to you until I embed it in your mind. Some people may refer to humans as being 'God's children', well, as fragments and sparks of love and light, you could say it's true, so the 'lesson' that follows is a 'children's' treat—but with a unique twist or two!

Imagine yourself as a small child, and in front of you stands the perfect sweet shop/candy store ... with large bay windows on either side of an old oak door. You are eager to enter this wondrous place, but thought you were not allowed, or in your heart, felt you didn't deserve to. Do not fear or worry any longer and acknowledge this choice has been—and always will be—your own.

Please understand, you do not need any currency within your pockets or purse dear child, for money has no place here. An exchange of energy like a Yen, Yuan, dollar, pound, and euro, or indeed any other 'coin' is not required. It is love, which is priceless, and cannot be measured by any sets of scales. Your own divine essence, which shines and illuminates inside—and all around you—demonstrates what you believe is your own self-worth. However, I can see beyond this, and therefore it is you who needs to comprehend your true value.

It's time to enter—and as you move forwards—a sign in golden light appears above the doorway ... 'ALL THINGS BRIGHT AND BEAUTIFUL'. You search for the handle, but there isn't one, because my heart to your one desire and goal is forever open to you all.

The oak door is ajar, and you walk inside. I immediately filled your senses with sweet fragrances, and the aroma of spices too, more than you could ever dream of. Your eyes light up, and your pulse races in the anticipation you can have anything you want or desire. There are many rows of 'candy' jars and shelf upon shelf of treats … and chocolate, too. But what is your favourite? Just pause for a moment in this childlike state, and think of what you would like, then try to sense the flavour right now.

Remember though, this is no traditional shop, and I am no 'Willy Wonka.' There is no counter here either because no barrier can ever divide you from me. You gaze upwards, and as a heavenly glow shines upon you, your heart skips a beat. Many questions enter your mind … "What is this? Is it magic? Are there really sweets in heaven? Wait … is that a 'galaxy', and what about those, are they bags of 'space dust' … aren't they 'flying saucers' too? Wow, is that 'Mars'? Hey … look at all those 'hundreds and thousands' shining brightly. Could that be a 'Milky Way'?"

In the search for answers, what you feel is beautiful. Your heart, mind and soul radiate and spiral within the amazing universe and creation, but this is not only a place where your body lives, as everything reflects the real you.

The earthly sweets, the ones your early years craved for, will soon be forgotten, leaving a bitter or sweet or even a sour flavour upon your taste buds. The tongue will no longer need to whet your appetite and try to fill your being, but instead, the essence and nectar I pollinate with my love— like a seed—becomes planted deep inside your soul. Then, by being 'still', the calmness; like a sea of tranquillity; will help this to flourish, and by cultivating and tending it with kindness and love, one's growth and understanding will thrive, not wither, and die.

Please appreciate, the chair on which you sit, inside the room of a house, in a village, town, city, and in any country upon Earth, as well as the planets, galaxies, space, 'time' and dimensions, are all part of the true sweetness of my love. All life is an expression, a thought, and a breath, and is all 'correct' and as they should be.

Therefore, do not imagine you are small or insignificant within the grand scheme of things. Likewise, let go of the 'I', which is your ego, and release all of your attachments. Here I do not mean you must sell all of your possessions, or give away everything you think you own, but erase what you say or think to yourself as 'mine'. Surrender all things and your love to me. When you truly hand over the reins of your life, you will never live in anxiety or fear. Do not be concerned or worried about what anyone else may think or do, for you are I and I am you.

Therefore, with this knowledge, let your imaginary hand reach out into the firmament. What will you choose? Would you catch a falling 'Starburst'? Or perhaps you just want to stop those 'space raiders' of negativity, doubt and despair! Whatever you think of, do not let the mind trick you, but always act in truth from the heart.

Okay, your brief stay is ending, but you can revisit whenever you wish. You are always welcome to the wisdom and this reality throughout the 'pick and mix' of life's experiences you find yourself in. You smile now, as your heart is more joyous and freer to shine brighter than it did before.

As you are about to pass back through the door, there is a 'love heart' (sweet) waiting for you as an extra gift. Before you pop it into your mouth, what word(s) are written upon it? The first thing your consciousness reveals is my message today … just for you.

You are now leaving the door behind you, but you pause to glance over your shoulder. The sign has now changed. Within a golden glow, you read, 'THE LORD GOD MADE THEM ALL!' Amen.

LESSON 23:

FRUSTRATION

Once again, sit and try to become still, even if you're ill at ease with yourself, because of the challenges of the day. It is quite possible these feelings arise with anxiety, fear, and anger, which all impress the mind.

In fact, each one of you will have moments of stress and angst, some daily, but for others, less frequently. It is vital you pause and reflect upon these times in order to counteract them, and let frustration fall away like removing a garment of clothing. In most instances where you cannot control the cause, know you can certainly change the 'effect'.

Remember, a mind is fickle and easily led astray from its normal thought process. Therefore, impose your own will through loving and positive thoughts, so it does not cause the tongue or body to inflict pain on another person or being. Understand, what you say or how you act will almost certainly be caused by a lack of control in the belief you cannot force your own desire—or outcome—upon someone else or even a particular task at hand.

Often during your life, one's frustration may encourage you to deny me, or make you think I abandon you to struggle alone. This will never be the case, but like any parent who wishes to guide and nurture their children, I do not complete your every task for you.

Comprehend, you can achieve anything and everything if you believe and work in truth, though I did not say only a single heart, or just one pair of hands (alone), would always accomplish it. Does a tailor provide the materials for the suits he makes? Do supermarkets grow their own food to sell? Does every petrol station make their own fuel for the vehicles on the road? Of course not, so those times when you want to give up, think you've had enough, or that the fun has disappeared, step back for a moment and reflect upon the experience itself.

Understand too, through time you will always learn, even far beyond the veil of life you call 'death'. Therefore, by attempting to learn any physical, emotional, or mental task, not only do you gain knowledge and through the 'action', but you also attain wisdom.

When faced with so-called difficulties, do not frown or despair, and no matter what you do or where you are, if you are trying your best, please forgive yourself. Likewise, forgiving others will also help release them from their own bondage of misgivings and mistrust. Each one of you can do this if you try, whether it's through encouraging words, an arm around another's shoulder, a smile or helping hand; for each is an act which stems from one heart to another.

People will often pray—or say—letting go is easier said than done, but do not forget I am with you and with you all. One must appreciate, a good deed can shine and illuminate both far and wide, sending joy along a vibration of hope and love. Likewise, when frustration is so intense, the anger, hatred and even revenge will cast shadows before you. In fact, until you let these feelings go, you take steps into uncertainty and doubt, and this creates the illusion you are actually on your own.

So, do not fear each passing day—when they seem to roll into one—but take vital time out, even for 10 minutes, to be true to you. Connect deep within to find the peace, stillness and calmness which often elude you. By doing this, especially when your mind cannot determine what you think is right or wrong, simply let go … and go with the flow.

If you cannot, life may seem like you are trying to paddle a canoe without an oar … upstream! But in reality, you need nothing else to guide you through the emotional waters of life, because I am the power, your essence, and divinity. Please understand this, so do not think you are a wave separate to the ocean, as I am your inner strength, your resolve, and the answer, always.

By letting me shine inside your heart, you will undertake many great things, and by recognizing you are I and I am you (self-realization), many of your so-called difficulties will ease and disappear. You will experience a new lease of life, because instinctively, it becomes easier for you to bear.

Your energy and vibration will elevate, as if a switch alters the current from negative to positive. The canoe—representing your vessel or body—will glide effortlessly, because my breath, like a gentle breeze, guides you forward into cleaner, clearer, and calmer waters.

Each day can be your own new beginning, as it can alter your attitudes toward the tasks in your life in a moment. If you feel weighed down by the expectation of home, work, or family responsibilities, think of those without a house in which to live, a job, or any next of kin. Change your mindset from wishing you did not have to mow the lawn, wash up, or clean, to one of gratitude for the roof over one's head, clothes to wear, food to eat, and even electricity and gas, as there are so many people who don't, even today.

Likewise, with one's workload, this is often self-inflicted because of the desire of impermanent possessions. Understand these are individual choices which can lead to exhaustion of the body and lack of time for those who you 'love'. Please try to do your job(s) for what help they can give to society and for those around you, but do not equate the hours of the day with the money to be earned, as further frustration can set in. Take on board the notion of working to the best of your ability, because there are those who would love to be the farmer, cleaner, shopkeeper, bin man, manager, scientist, scholar, or a so-called 'breadwinner'.

In addition, do not be annoyed or perplexed by family members, as many souls actually wish and pray for a brother, sister, mother, or father. Everyone —on the exterior—displays their faults, and when one highlights and picks upon another's, it is but a reflection of their own. You are all special, no matter what size, shape, and colour of your hair or skin, and therefore life should be lived and enjoyed, and you do not always need 'cash' to do that.

Realise those who live in darkness would be in ecstasy to sense the warmth and light of the Sun. Someone trapped by something—or someone —on a mental, emotional, or a physical level (held hostage), will truly know what it is like to be free. To those who long for a child, and then become parents, the gift is priceless. For the thirsty and hungry, a glass of water and a piece of bread are worth more than all the precious jewels of the world.

Of course, you can strive to reach your goals and achievements, but I request you to gain some balance in your lives. Indeed, what gratitude do you display or share? Are you content? Contentment eradicates frustration, and those 'push me-pull you' effects of your so-called ups and downs.

Remember too, all the answers lie within you, and the light 'hierarchy' of friends, family, teachers, spirit guides, angels and archangels work and help you all the time through the many hearts and hands of others.

Be aware that love is, was, and forever shall be. You are never without love, even when you wish to shout or tear your hair out, or if you think your mind is going to burst open. When this feeling rears its ugly head, simple things can ease difficult problems ... for instance, a breath of fresh air, listening to your favourite song, or being with someone or something close to your heart.

Finally, today, please do not give up your own aspirations or dreams, because we can overcome frustration. Remember, by playing your part and role in life with truth, you will win the ultimate prize of self-realization of your own divinity. Amen.

LESSON 24:

SILENCE

I am here, there, and everywhere. Therefore, I recognize and understand you every second, minute, and hour of the day. However, because of the way most people live their lives, they do not know me, because their minds become agitated, or their senses—in demise—obscure the truth. Some of you may think these words are harsh, abrupt, or even condescending, but look beyond them, into their meaning and explanation.

Regarding today's 'lesson', many of you will state they can see, but one must appreciate it is not just the sense of sight which leads to 'insight'. For instance, picture a scene of the sea, gently washing upon the shoreline, or the stars glistening within a clear night sky, as both are visual treats. These images often evoke peace, harmony, and the yearning for knowledge about what, why and how you are a part of creation.

For all this, true vision will not reveal itself through physical eyes alone. You need to comprehend that your brain and mind will try to decipher, reason, and substantiate their purpose by utilising sight and other senses, too. So, you must bypass or short circuit the thoughts they generate, which allows you to become conscious of me. When you can re-focus through the lens of 'truth and wisdom'—with, to and through your heart's centre—the information and answers you require are revealed.

I will project reality towards you like beacons of hope and joy, for they act as a two-way mirror. In viewing this, you not only see your own reflection, but I see you, too. This is the reason you cannot hide, run away, or become isolated, though please remember … the mind attempts to justify everything, and therefore imparts both doubt and fear. In contrast, you can help yourself by removing the clutter of mental noise, to leave a clean canvass for growth, understanding, wisdom and peace!

Sometimes it only takes a small change in your habits or conduct with whom you meet, and by what you do or say. This, in turn, can alter your plans, hopes and dreams positively—if you let them. Only in silence can you hear your own truth and what 'I' am saying to you. It is not enough to turn the television or radio off, as you must control the wandering mind. By taking charge of the senses, you are not only acknowledging this fact, but at the same time, you become aware of me and your own divinity.

One must appreciate that no exterior solution—to manipulate or exploit another's life and true purpose—will ever be found. In addition, within the silence of your heart, no amount of external or internal 'chatter' will affect the reality of you. Know the answers you seek are here and here alone.

Over time, you'll familiarize yourself with the way your mind—working through your senses—sways you from side to side, not unlike walking into a blustery gale. By continually moving forward with the correct intentions, you'll comprehend exactly whom and where you are right now, and how the silence can bring clarity and focus through the right action of your being too. Every one of you has a choice, no matter what level you are working on. You can carry on as you are, or you can start to make a difference to your life and surroundings.

Please understand, your energy and love will shine brighter if you share these from within your heart and soul. Not all gifts cost money, and as I said before, even a smile or helping hand can change another's opinion or make them feel appreciated and thought of. This is self-perpetuating, for when you feel good you can do 'good', but only with the correct intentions and purpose. It is not ego centred, but through love where truth in action materializes, across space, time, and all dimensions.

What should I say or do next, in order to advise or assist you further in these matters? Would you like me to move mountains of karmic debt, worry, fear, hatred, and anger? Or will the penny drop, in the realization each one of you can reach beyond the stars, without the limitations and boundaries you yourselves had set.

As previously mentioned, my love has manifested itself within a physical embodiment too, some of which have been called an Avatar. Every appearance reignites the flame inside you all, to assist and help you illuminate through the word and action of truth. Of course, some will not sense these bodily incarnations as a reflection of me, but no matter, as your goal is to bear witness to the light and wisdom through your own heart.

Remember, these 'bodies', past and present, are only a ripple upon the waters of human emotion, which I send to change oneself, your communities and society around the world. By connecting on the exterior and also within thyself, my breath, which is the very air you inhale and exhale, will enable you to refocus on the 'Sai-lens'. (This refers both to silence and to Sai Baba of India, who will forever be known as the Avatar of this age). Your love will then become magnified beyond all recognition.

Through your continued journey, you will realise peace and stillness have many additional purposes. For example, it enables one to withdraw from the impermanent world in which you currently live. Another is the opportunity to connect with the frequency of your inner thoughts, and not the constant barrage of the 'lower' mind, which links so tirelessly to your senses, and attempts to bind you with the gratification of unrefined energy and vibrations, to and of the body.

Within truth, there is peace, bliss, and everlasting joy, so we can relate this to your real or higher 'self'. You may also know these as the soul or Atma, two words to name but a few. You do not need to travel to faraway destinations and cross deserts or seas to acknowledge this, for I am in all places.

Together, we are one … so please discover me through your heart's stillness. Then, the clarity of true vision, alongside the elements of the sky— ether—air, fire, water, and earth, will all manifest more easily for, from, through and to you. I stated before, everything you say, think or do is the choice through your own desires, though I will never tire of guiding, helping, encouraging, and protecting you in your life.

Even in your darkest hour, I am with you. You are never alone. Though you often view your experiences as a hindrance, try to live your days knowing that I bless you with my grace and my love to help you. Overall, silence can be your new beginning, but it will never be your end! Amen.

LESSON 25:

PAIN

I welcome every heart and soul, to not only read or hear these words, but sense them inside of you too. In doing so, the title of this lesson pierces the mind, and may bring heavy sighs of what is coming, but do not be afraid, or even imagine a never-ending period of loss or separation, either.

As the Sun shines and beams its rays of light and warmth upon the Earth, so does my love, which glistens and radiates for every being, soul, and all life. With the wind, my breath washes over your face, and through the water you drink, I quench your thirst. Within the soil, I cultivate nutrients for your body, and inside your heart I am the 'love' beating fast or slow … leading, guiding, forgiving, and willing you to grow.

Each of your memory's floats like a butterfly's wings and soft whispers from times of old, and your soul can seem far away upon distant shores. In reality, no one can remember who, what or where he or she has come from, or been. Only the realization of a once held destiny remains clear, deep within all creation.

Therefore, know with certainty I have captured your hearts. Moreover— please understand—it is each one of you who holds mine. In fact, my essence and divinity lie inside every leaf, rock, moon, star, and galaxy, and inside all life itself, held in place by the greatest power of all … 'love'.

How can a four-letter word convey something so powerful? Well, first, love contains everything. It is the light and the dark. It is hope and fear. It is freedom or a prison, and joy, bliss, or pain. One must realise love and hate go hand in hand too, so do not divide or say this isn't so, as all will fail.

Deep inside you, this power beckons to be released. Sometimes it trickles to the surface, or cascades like fountains and waterfalls from eyes and hearts. When your tears fall, they resonate and glisten, resembling dew upon snowdrops in brilliant sunshine. They can sparkle like snowflakes, captured by moonlight on cold frosty nights, or sing softly, as gentle lullabies to a new-born child. Comprehend and distinguish this as the power and glory— but also the pain.

As each second goes by on the 'earth-plane', I express life in billions of ways via body, mind, and soul. Regarding the physical, if burnt, cut, beaten, or neglected, you will feel it in various degrees and levels, unless the mind is incapacitated. In contrast, mental pain can arise from misunderstanding, frustration, and indecision, or by toxins released from—or through—the body.

Then, there is emotional pain of the heart and soul, which is worst of all, as it may never seem to heal. Cries ring out from across every land and throughout all time through what most call a 'loss', a separation, or death. For each one of you, there is no greater fear, but despite this, it is the one mountain to climb and overcome in order to find the truth.

Remember, I bear witness to everything, including the stillborn child laying in a mother's arms, or the disappearance of a beloved next of kin or pet, seemingly vanished, as if into thin air. I sense all pain, emitted like arrows or spears from screaming hearts, or those deafened in silence and despair.

Please listen carefully—and try to understand—in your deepest, darkest hour, you may disown, ask, tell, or shout at me over why I did not help or intervene. Know this query is but a veil, trying to cover love in a shadow of doubt, along with anger as a cloak of mystery.

Appreciate all lives is a lesson, and you are experiencing and living because you are 'creation' in 'action'. You are energy, you are love, and I connected all in an unbroken link to each other and to me ... for we are 'one', as I constantly reiterate to you.

Understand our love does not hide or pretend to another, and one cannot fake tears of true joy or pain. In the moments of immense grief, the mind is oblivious to exterior words, but the heart—torn in two—will become one again. I promise you that this will unclench your fists, and even though you imagine you might succumb to such pain, I am the glue and the light to mend what you believe is non-repairable.

Never think you are alone either or think your loved one has 'gone'—not to be seen again—because you are living on a lower, denser vibration, that is all. Love is always closer than you think. They are no more than being in the next room, behind a false door without a handle. A special key or password is not required to open it. You just need to accept you cannot be reunited ... because it does not separate you! These feelings are but notions in the mind or words upon lips you don't yet understand, but you will.

No matter how difficult something is, or how much you wish a large hole would come and swallow you up, try with all your power to hold on to the connection and the love between two hearts. This is your strength; it is never a weakness.

Comprehend too, throughout your life there will be the so-called good or bad times, but refrain from calling them this. It is only experience, but this brings knowledge and wisdom. Therefore, in suffering pain, you should know you are actually stronger, not weaker, and upon a soul level, you will never, ever go through more than you can truly bear.

If you believe and trust in yourself, you believe and trust in me, too. By trusting me implicitly—in particular with what you deem as desperate times —your heart will recognize I have not forsaken you, and that I love you more deeply and more fondly than you could ever imagine!

However, when you deny me, my love oozes like blood from an open wound, and when you reject yourself and the reality within, my 'heart' aches. I want it to burst open, showering the Earth in a rainfall of tears.

In fact, pain needs to fade between man and nature, and man versus man, because love will heal all beings. Every one of you can help to change the world. You only need to live, breathe, and believe it to be so. Overall, no matter how painful life seems, there can be real growth through your endeavours when you think, hope, and desire the truth. Amen.

LESSON 26:

DEBRIS

As the connection between love and light guides the pen, I now welcome you with these thoughts and words. Please comprehend the ink, which glides across the page, is only an impression made in wet sand. Therefore, will the teaching of such lessons remain within your heart and soul, or blur and fade, washed away by the tides of your emotions?

In all sacred texts and 'written word' throughout time, every consonant, vowel, phrase, sentence, paragraph, and book, resonate at their own frequency. Because of this, their understanding remains fixed, resembling deep-rooted trees, or they float like feathers and leaves upon the breeze. Therefore, if one's vibrational state matches the energy of what they read or heard, then the information, knowledge, and wisdom become easier to digest, as the recognition of truth falls into place.

In contrast, sometimes the young or old—no matter what their colour or nationality—will place it to one side until a new day dawns. Everything has its time, place, and purpose, so an individual's learning cannot be forced or rushed … wisdom arrives precisely when it is meant to. If this were not the case, it would be like a new-born baby studying for a degree or scholarship.

All spiritual guidance and education work this way, and the seeker, aspirant, devotee—or whatever name you care to place or describe this search and quest for truth—will realise this. Every one of you is resonating and working on different levels of transition within your hearts, minds, and souls … but one cannot say they are any better or have progressed further than another.

Appreciate too, the current bodily incarnation you each possess is not affected in this way. The soul resonates and illuminates, not by another's thoughts or actions, but of its own accord and power within. It is the same with all karma/karmic debt. As such, your brother, sister, mother, father or any other next of kin cannot erase or clear past deeds carried out by yourself.

One could call these things your soul's debris, the fallout from the illusion and confusion over many millennia. This takes a persona of many forms and guises, and along with bruised egos, there is the physical, mental, spiritual, and ethereal pain, or someone who displays a spoiled character and personality, a real Jekyll and Hyde.

Even so, things differ from previous generations, and those eras of time, which drifted by upon the 'earth-plane'. This is because I give you an opportunity and a gift—from my heart to yours—and during this 'age', every being and soul, across billions of worlds within time and space, can all reduce or erase what they require inside.

Simply put, through your own self-realization, you can attain your eternal happiness and joy. This is no game of pretence, by somehow brushing the debris under a carpet, or trying to disguise the truth of past lives or deeds. No, this is permanent, for I place my loving heart around every spark of divinity to cleanse the negativity, angst, fear, and pain from the plumes and flame of your true self.

In this moment, bliss and peace will shine eternally, allowing you all to witness and experience my love. The tears of your soul will cascade like crystal waterfalls throughout my kingdom … knowing that love reigns supreme, formed in recognition that you are born of love, remain free by love, and forever will be loved.

Many call such events 'ascension'; this is fine, though this indicates a 'coming from' and a 'going to' scenario. In fact, you already are, were, and always will be part of me … in whatever form or appearance the soul takes. Try to comprehend, the soul has been magnetized because of the bodily senses and lack of mind control. This attracted debris over the passages of time, by false fear, desire, hate, anger, jealousy, and so much more from misguided and trapped negative thoughts, words, and deeds.

Through your endeavours and expansion of truth and light, the polarity will change. The acts of compassion, forgiveness and joy dissipate and transform negativity across time and space, and through love, a shift across the Earth's population will alter from selfishness and doubt to selflessness and a certainty we are all one.

Your frequency of divinity will radiate like iron filings upon a piece of paper, and I am the new magnet which attracts you in waves of rainbows and colours more beautiful than you could ever imagine. Understand too, I am the pot of true gold that awaits you all, but you do not need to use any man-made appliance to detect where I am, though you must still dig deeper than you have ever tried before. No spades or shovels are required … only the quest for your own truth inside you. When you know thyself, you'll know me. In knowing 'I am I', you will appreciate all of creation is at your disposal and should be used.

No matter whom or where you are, understand this opportunity knocks for you all. Please trust in yourself, and therefore trust in me—as I often reiterate to you—because each burden of your incarnations, I will bear for you … but do you believe me? Do you think I can do this for you? Is a leap of faith really required when you fully comprehend that I am all life? You alone must answer this question.

It is important to comprehend your reality in this lifetime. If you cannot, or do not wish to change or grow—within the light—I shall not forsake you. Your soul's path—which you set—will continue, of course, because, as always, these choices are your own. Some may wonder or beg to question, "Well, why bother with this so-called opportunity or amnesty then?" I reply and simply state, I love you all … and by using earthly connotations, nine out of ten people would never look a gift horse in the mouth. Please believe there has been no coercion, but I know what is best for each 'life' in all scenarios, throughout every dimension.

Upon the 'earth-plane' at this time, much conflict and heartache persist. Mother Nature is often frustrated with floods, fires, and many other means by which to express her 'being'. Through all these situations and experiences or tests, humankind endures and can become strengthened, with many shining brighter than ever before. Like a patchwork quilt or blanket, you are each a segment, connecting and playing out their part to expand the consciousness of love and light.

Therefore, to summarize this lesson: your souls are like comets and asteroids which collected small or large pieces of dirt and debris, becoming darker with every new bodily overcoat that's worn. I promise to steer you away from these never-ending cycles, where perceived mistakes are repeated.

My love will guide you through the restless atmosphere of many eras, so you may become shooting stars, burning away karmic dust and grime to reveal your eternal brightness of a thousand or billion Suns. As such, the permanent bliss of peace awaits you, always and forever within my heart. Amen.

LESSON 27:

LIMITS

The aim of this lesson is to help the reader, aspirant, or devotee focus and understand whether any boundaries or self-imposed restrictions have been set within their lives. It should become apparent that many opportunities simply pass you by; like leaves falling unnoticed from the trees, or because the mind has been destabilised through medication or illness. In fact, it becomes quite clear most people feel inhibited, or lack confidence in attaining or fulfilling their hopes, dreams, and goals, but why is this?

Well, one may think there are those who own the right—or the power—to deny someone else's achievements, or that society and the way of general 'living' can lead people to believe a parent, teacher, or any governing body has jurisdiction and authority over an outcome. On the surface, this might seem the case, and even such things as being shy and withdrawn, or having no conviction or ability, could be the reason. However, please brush aside these notions, for if truth be told, the very cause is the 'self', not listening to one's own intuition or conscience.

In every walk of life—and it doesn't matter whether you are male or female and young or old—sometime or somewhere you have said, "I can't do that", or "I don't actually deserve this". As I have described many times before, you are each a divine spark and essence of me, and therefore, why do you still believe you cannot achieve your goals and ambitions? Do you think you are unworthy and unable to bring forth thy hopes and dreams to fruition?

Though the subject of karma has been discussed frequently before—and the part this plays—more often than not, it is one's own negativity or lack of determination and perseverance which cannot materialize your wishes. I know this because I am the eternal witness, and from the moment you wake, you plan and use bodily senses to implement your thoughts. For instance, the clothes you wear and the food you eat, the route you decide to take to work, who to talk to, and what tasks need completing … the list seems endless. In reality, what is the difference in manifesting the outcome of these events compared to your spiritual education and self-realization?

You also plan holidays, outings, or trips, with military precision regarding luggage, transport, and the 'currency' to spend, while not forgetting to make sure one's home or any pets are safe and secure. There appears no limit to the effort involved, and they nearly all come to their fruition. So, if one can achieve all this, then surely the ability to move those so-called 'mountains' is within you too ... through your belief, courage, fortitude and love.

Obviously, determination plays an important factor, because there are many roads littered with aspirations, while the hopes and dreams park in the recesses of the mind, just like vehicles stopped in their tracks, having run out of fuel. One must realise this reduction of energy—through the body—might be tiredness, or an absence of will power. The first is easily remedied with rest, relaxation, and a decrease of stress in your life. The second forms part of your character, which may be more difficult to change ... if change is what you require.

Sometimes during childhood, I bear witness to a lack of discipline or encouragement from parents towards a child, and perhaps this is an inherited trait. But no matter what age you are within your bodily incarnation, I hope to lead you forward into a new period of your life, so do not think you are ever a failure, or believe another when they say you will not amount to anything. In addition, do not fear failing to scale the heights of one's so-called peers. I tell you these things, not to highlight any weakness, but because I love you.

As I am you and you are me—the light, the way, and the truth—then you must start to see your future through different lenses. Many will state that an ambition, goal, or the desire for reality is like looking through rose-tinted glasses ... this is not the case, for if you look too and from and through your heart, you bear witness to the victory of all battles, which is over 'Self'.

Therefore, do not feel you compete with any other person, be it friend, foe, or brother, because the fight is only inside yourself. Then, as you become more in tune and accustomed to this process of evolvement, you will understand there are no limits to my power at all, and hence, deep within you lies the reflection of me.

Okay, I mentioned your character earlier, well ... one should refrain from judging someone else's, lest you yourself be 'judged'. It is only another's opinion whether they think you are good, bad, or indifferent, so try not to live life comparing yours with another. Remember, even those who live in those so-called ivory towers will attempt to maintain their imperfect exterior traits—which become displayed within the impermanent world—but only their soul's divine essence is pure.

As such, do not say or even think, "He—or she—is better (or worse) than me", because only negativity manifests and displays itself from utilizing these words or thoughts. It would be wise to acknowledge your own situation within society as a human being, and whether you are the best that you can be.

Remember, life is full of twists, turns, opportunities and openings, with choices and dreams from the cradle to the grave, so do not look back into the past with regrets. You cannot change it. Likewise, the future is only the seeds sown in the present. So, please do this with love and care in the ploughed furrows of truth—inside your heart—in the knowledge they will grow and flourish there, because my love will radiate upon them. The foundation of your ambitions becomes nourished and sustained by the fountain of tears from my joy.

Over time, love which flows to and through and from you—with your own efforts—will shine forth like a flower bud opening on a warm sunny day. Within you, the plumes of your eternal fire will glisten and sparkle like open petals caught by a shower of rain in the hot summer sun. You then display your magnificence for evermore, as you finally understand that your own brilliance is without limitation.

At all levels of vibration and energy you currently reside upon, it is only the illusion, your self-doubt, and the constant stream of other's self-denial—of whom and what you all are—which both inhibits and detracts you from each individual's correct path. Therefore, any boundaries and limits you set are not—and never will become—imposed by me. Therefore, you reach out with your hands and words of prayer because you understand I am limitless, which forms the fabric of your very being.

Acknowledging this will enable you to unpick those crossed stitches of negativity and despair, to pick up the thread and invisible cord which connects us all. It is of one connection and destiny, and an everlasting source of bliss and peace, forever and a day. Amen.

LESSON 28:

THE WORLD

For some of you, being able to focus upon the joy and love in the world right now might be difficult … due to 'devastation' as recent earthquakes and tsunamis. These events captivate the media around the globe, who display these scenes and images bringing tears of further suffering and anguish to millions, but within this technological and modern age in which you live, it is easy to become blinded and bound by conflict, war, destruction, and pain.

Please do not feel this lesson will divert attention away from these things, or imagine I am requesting you to ignore any small or great need of another life—whether they are near or far—either by your thoughts and prayers, or through physical action or deeds.

In such times, it is important to remove any obstacles obstructing the truth being relayed. So, similarly to removing a thorn from the flesh, you must eradicate the splinter of confusion and illusion from the 'I' (Self). Once separated, there is instant relief, and instead of blurred or narrow vision, you experience clarity with body, mind, and soul in unison, as 'one'.

Therefore, it is my purpose today, to help you remember to change the way you think, to rewind and re-focus one's thoughts towards love and light, because negativity and fear of death or disease try to drive you away from me. Please understand, my connection to you can't be broken, and so your divine essence will steer you toward truth—like a pigeon whose instinct enables it to return home—for your heart belongs to me, and vice versa.

The link between us is not a contract or an arrangement between two parties. We are not separate. Also, each of your sojourns (soul-journeys), within different bodily garments, are so brief to me, like the blink of your eye. In fact, your life can be captivated and expressed in a single heartbeat, but even so, it provides you with a glorious opportunity to experience the world … achieving self-realization, glory, and bliss of true peace.

Perhaps then, during your busy life, you can pause and reflect even for a short while … to think and recall happier times and events, those which magically lift your heart. What experiences—etched deep within the mind— now shine from your soul? A memory can stay with you—like a page in a book with its corner creased—so that you do not forget that special place or face? What photograph captivates and ignites the spark inside you? What words, text, expression, or emotion inspired you, helping you to fulfil your dreams?

One should bask in knowledge, truth, and the beautiful sights and sounds which surround you all, but most people become far too busy to see, hear, or sense them within. Please ask yourself, "Do I now have time to spare, and therefore appreciate the wonders of living in this world?" Ninety-nine out of one hundred people would say yes, but the opportunities still come and go and are so readily missed.

To help you contemplate and realise what I mean, perhaps you could open your heart, soul, and mind to those memories of your own, and the images and scenes of the world these next few words portray to you. Whether you are single, married, or have ever been in a relationship, can you not recall experiences such as these?

Your first kiss.

Your wedding day.

The first time you made love.

The birth of your child.

Your first job.

A sunrise or sunset.

The stars sparkling in a clear night sky.

A Brilliant rainbow.

An embrace from a long-forgotten friend.

Your body, and the abilities and senses you think you do or do not possess.

The air you breathe.

Mother Nature.

A snowflake.

The glow of a full moon.

A flower.

Rain.

Freedom.

The comfort of your home in whatever shape or form.

Food and water.

Your ability to forgive and heal relationships.

Love.

Each of the above will mean different things to different people, but all can relate to them. Of course, one can take many things in life for granted. It can become second nature, whereby you do not appreciate or even bear witness to a beautiful scene or the experience which passes you by ... only to fade away into the impermanent world.

Though this continually takes place, try to understand that within your soul, one immense difference must occur. But what is it? Well, it is the link of love and light which cannot change or ever be erased, and all creation contains this 'energy' of me. Therefore, this truth binds us together, forming innumerable and immeasurable chains to connect all life.

Appreciate the Earth is precious. Those who are fortunate to have viewed the planet from space say its beauty is almost impossible to describe. In fact, the world you live upon may seem to rest—almost alone—against a backdrop of stars, but please comprehend, it is one of billions across time and many dimensions, where the echoes of my breath touches and connects each and all as one.

For that reason, the chair in which you sit, placed inside the room of your home, set in the village, town, or city, within the country, nation, and continent, are all connected elements. Do not feel I am contradicting myself through these words, for some may say, "How can the world be so vital if there is no individuality?" I would simply reply, well there are billions of you, aren't there? No one is less important than another.

Understand there are millions of planets with habitable life too. Scientists and astrologers use telescopes, or gaze over pictures via satellites, and yet, what they currently see is leaving the 'unseen' behind. Are they invisible? No. Is this the truth? Yes. Realise there is a veil which distorts their vision, which resembles looking through frosted glass, because sight using one's eyes alone is not enough.

Therefore, one may state the question, "If there is life on other worlds, are they treasured too?" Of course, they are, but it is vital to appreciate how special the Earth is to you, not me. Only when people fully appreciate the ground they walk upon as being sacred and a privilege, and an experience and divine opportunity to express your love to all life with contentment, will peace then ensue.

I can only help you through your helping yourselves. Not because I won't or can't, but because it is through your own inner divinity, acceptance and understanding which will unite all sparks of light into one flame of truth. Do not be mistaken or believe these last few words appear to divide you, for they do not. The world's population may think they are apart and differ from each other; so, I therefore need to highlight and express this in these terms, so you find the way forward together.

There is so much for everyone to be positive about, and you can shine the way your light is supposed to. Remember, 'be' in the world, but gain your true strength from 'within', becoming resolute and determined to overcome the doubt and anxiety which may come your way. Recognize the real beauty is inside you, and this will manifest around the globe … so try to fulfil your potential and not waste the time you have been pre-sent and given to you.

I love you all. If you can love yourself, you will love all life, and the world will change. Indeed, the rising of emotional waters will subside, anger will dissipate, eruptions shall disappear. Indeed, those clouds of toxic and violent 'energy' will no longer threaten, but disperse, leaving a cleaner, purer atmosphere for all to live and breathe. Believe it, and it will be so. Amen.

LESSON 29:

SPRINGTIME

As you sit in silence, I remind you once more of the tranquillity and peace both within and out. One must realise you will never find this when the body and mind are racing about, and the expression "running around like headless chickens" comes to the fore. Therefore, try to imagine you are in a garden once more, and as the spring sunshine feels like a blessing, a clear blue sky creates an ambience and serenity which seems to drift down upon you. While there, birds float effortlessly on the 'wing', whilst others sit and sing magical notes resembling sweet lullabies.

Many people sense springtime as a new beginning, with flower bulbs rising to the surface, and the daffodils opening to the Sun. Similarly, everywhere you look for truth, you know this is flourishing too. As many souls emerge from the shade and shadows of doubt and confusion, they become aware it is a dawn of the new age, because fresh connections and links of light are radiating from country to country and continent to continent, which brings true friendship, compassion, and love.

One ought to instil these same traits, both inside and outside the home. Like the rooks and crows who fly with twigs and other necessities to build their nests in lofty treetops, they only use what is required. Similarly, one should only feather their own nest with what is essential to sustain the body, mind, and soul.

Only the individual can decree what these are, but I implore you not to become attached to impermanent or unnecessary things. It is not your life's purpose to accumulate and keep possessions with a fear of losing them. This will only entrap you with anxiety, worry, and needless thoughts of negativity, which will often spiral out of control.

Right now, though, the rays of the sunshine brighter, and they fill you with a warm, magical glow. Looking down towards your feet, you see a lone buttercup peering up between the blades of grass. It moves slightly in the breeze, creating a shimmer of golden yellow which captivates your eyes. Isn't that amazing?

Breathing in the fresh air is a privilege not all can experience, so these simple things can make one appreciative of being alive. Suddenly a thought flashes across your mind, 'How lucky am I'. Well, understand I am fully aware and drawn to those contented hearts who give thanks, but do not judge me here, for I am within every heart.

The reason I mention this is that many people still deny me, and in doing so, they only deny themselves. Again, please know I love you all, but it is difficult for some to express my love through their hearts, captivated or restrained by the impermanent world around them.

Also, one must not assume I require—or have ever needed—any of you to shower gifts upon statues which you believe depict who I am. These things form many of your traditions and faiths around the globe—having been passed or handed down from generation to generation—so you must always do what you think is right inside you.

Understand that the only sacrifice someone needs to make is to set me free ... to do my 'divine' will—not thy will—but what on earth do I mean? Well, I am held captive within every element of life, so if you do not release me, how can I let my love flow with your own? We are 'one' remember?

Therefore, opening your soul to new ways of thinking and being is like breaking ice upon the sea. Picture an icebreaker, a ship which enables safe passage for others to follow ... as you are these vessels, I can only clear the path before you on my ocean of love, and if you understand we are inseparable within this 'oneness', love will flow effortlessly too.

I realise you often come against situations in your life where you think you are banging your head against a brick wall. These are the times when you are not letting me work through you, but if you were to trust in me and yourself, you will know there is no ice too thick, which we cannot break. No matter what challenges or difficulties you face, I am with you. You are never alone—as I keep reiterating—and if you ever think you are; it is only because an outside influence has tricked your mind.

Okay, while pausing for a moment within this garden, savour the senses and wonder about the glory of it all, as this energy about you so enchanting. In such stillness and peace, the sights and sounds of animals, birds and insects bring an oasis of calm ... Mother Nature is so beautiful, do you not agree?

The Sun feels even warmer and brighter now, and the sunshine reflects off the ladybird's backs—like mirrors—as they rest upon the wooden log nearby. Yes, so much life seems to awaken around you, and wherever you are to sense it, by knowing this reality in your heart, everything else will follow.

In your life, there is always something always you need to do. There are places to be and people to meet, but please find time to contemplate and be 'still'. Do not worry about the past ... your yesterday. Be aware not to be driven too much by the future either. All that matters is now, the present ...

pre-sent to you, and this gift of 'time'—and what you do within the moment —is more precious and important than you can know.

When you are in this stillness, one could say, I am happy. By sensing me, the stars appear to dazzle, and your hearts sparkle more beautifully than all the diamonds and so-called prized jewels of the world. These moments are unforgettable. They become etched within your soul's memories forever and a day, and no earthly price can ever be placed upon them.

Always remember, it is vital to create a balance in your life and one's work, rest, and play. Do not live with head and mind in the clouds either, for anyone who neglects his kith and kin, or home cannot function properly. Being spiritual and aspirant or devotee of truth does not require you to live in a cave, or by erasing the connections from those who love you.

This may sound like a record player, or an iPod on 'repeat', but I will always 'replay' what and when is meant to be read—or heard—at the correct time and place. So then, what will you do with the rest of your day or evening? What words, actions, or thoughts will emanate from inside you? Please know you can achieve so much with the right attitude, belief, and by sharing the love and truth from your heart.

I can, and will help you, if you let me. With no force—or coercion—nothing is impossible in, to, through, and from love. With certainty, this springtime heralds another opportunity to grow in strength and kindness, so leave any winter blues in the dullness of the night.

Let us take flight together as you are my other wing, and we will soar higher and further than you ever thought or dreamt possible. You can never fly too near the 'Son', as love's rays only beckon you to shine more intensely and brightly—each day or lifetime—than you have ever done before. Some may say the sky is the limit, but in truth, it is not even the start. Understand, deep within you; our love is for eternity ... forever, world without end. Amen.

LESSON 30:

ACCEPTANCE OF SELF

Welcome once again. Before we begin this guidance today, it would prove helpful to pause and reflect upon the title of the lesson. In doing so, you may wonder what acceptance means, and whether it can be beneficial regarding your interaction with others. In addition, one might consider how this trait could affect your life and lifestyle from here on in.

Indeed, there is a lot to contemplate and discuss on the matter, however, priority has to be with yourself and you alone, because even though you all vary in size, shape, and tone of skin, character, and personality, there may well be something you cannot accept or tolerate at this time.

Upon your rebirth into the material world, one appears to resemble a blank canvass—naked and sometimes blue—but please understand, beyond DNA and your physicality lies so much more than the eye can see … or what the heart is yet to convey. From a babe in arms, there will be karma to balance and many experiences to share and partake too, in order for you to grow spiritually, physically, mentally, and emotionally.

I have discussed this on countless occasions before, but all these things will leave a trace within the heart, mind, and soul. In fact, you could actually describe it as a revelation, and an opportunity for growth and expansion of one's light and resonance.

Therefore, as each day dawns, an array of tasks is due to be accomplished, which uses all your time and energy. Every single one of you must appreciate those best laid plans can go awry; yet you still become frustrated, which can perplex the mind. In such circumstances, what do—or do you not —accept?

How often do you think someone, something, or even the entire world is against you? How many yells of, "Why me?" must one scream? Please try to rise above these times, in the knowledge each second, minute or hour presents you with a chance to live in the moment. Why must the outcome of whatever tasks you undertake, and the results of thought, word, and deed become even better, more easily achieved, continually striving for so-called perfection?

People are usually concerned with what others say, think or do, but if you try your best from the heart and soul, then they must accept both you and the resulting outcome. Remember, if there are purity and conviction from within, all consequences I will endure as my burden and gift to you.

Earlier, I mentioned the 'physical', which plays a major role in your life. People often interpret this as being an acceptance of another person, whether they are fat, thin, tall, or small and with different colour skin, hair and eyes, etcetera. However, it is not what—or how—someone else sees you, but it is how you perceive and feel about yourself.

It is vital for you to accept who and what you are, and not just one's physical appearance, but spiritually, too. Again, do not confuse this with any religion or faith, because an acceptance of your own divinity and of 'self' is twofold.

The first of which concerns your own appearance, because it is important to maintain a healthy lifestyle. You can then focus on your true 'well-being' and purpose. Do not hanker after someone else's looks, or imagine you are less worthy than those with wealth, because money is fickle. It can disappear, be lost, taken away, and eroded. Realise your character and reputation are worth far more to me, and to you.

In time, you must accept one's looks fade, hair turns to grey, skin will crinkle, and no amount of makeup can hide the truth of age. From the moment of your physical birth, the clock is ticking. So—through acceptance of yourself—you can achieve a great deal in your life. Time is not then wasted on being something you are not or trying to portray a picture of someone who you think others wish to see.

Second, regarding your own divinity, can you accept this as being true or not? Of course, many countless millions will state they are born, they live, and then they die … nothing more and nothing less. Please appreciate, I do not love those—who feel this way—any differently from any other soul.

Comprehend only that by denying me … they are also denying themselves. This creates false barriers which attempt to stop them from experiencing my love to, through, and from one's heart. By taking one-step towards me in thought and word and deed, I take many more towards you. This is not a bargaining chip, a contract, or a 'special' deal I only offer to a select few, but a simple fact.

Imagine a lamp shining in the darkness. From a distance, it is just a flicker, and offers no distinguishable features to the eyes of the body or heart. If you draw closer, this light will shine upon a clearer path, helping, guiding, and willing you onwards for your journey. Like a lighthouse, I can steer you clear of unnecessary harm and ease you through the turbulent waves of your emotions.

By accepting you are not just a 'body', you can navigate through the ups and downs of your life. Treat each day with equanimity. You will also understand you are not the 'doer', but the vessel with which to experience and grow. Therefore, do not fear, thinking you have no control. So, throughout your life, you must continue to make choices and decisions that will not only affect yourself, but of loved ones and others around you, too. Again, an acceptance, but also one of responsibility.

In all things, you still have to accept the possibility there can be consequences for your actions, for one cannot hide from cause and effect. Each action is like a ripple upon still waters, and they both dissipate and blend into the pool of life, or start those radiating rings of discontent, felt far beyond the initial displacement and impact. So, where does this take you now?

Please answer truthfully, with the knowledge every day can be a new beginning and a challenge for all. So, what difference can you now make? Remember, even a smile has positive side effects and shines your light far greater than you may think. As such, do you wake up thinking each day is going to be the same … or with gratitude, for a new morning to share the reality of you?

Of course, there will be times when you are so low and think you do not know which way to turn, but this is precisely when you need to withdraw into stillness, to find the answers, and connect with your love and light. Please ask me to guide and help you show the way forward, because when you cannot give anymore, and believe you have tried everything else you can, you will understand I am taking over the reins.

I work through you, but only if you want me to. I will carry your burdens and lighten your load … and lead you to the outcome of truth—and the results will be in my hands. Remember, if your heart seems to have taken you as far as it will go, then do not fear, worry, or shed tears of pain or anguish, because accepting my strength with true conviction can move mountains and help you achieve your dreams!

Comprehend too, the person next to you in the car, bus, train, boat, or plane may appear different on the outside, but inside, only the brightness varies. Please appreciate this, the body's appearance can be very deceiving. Th so-called 'down and out' on the side of the road can be far more than you could ever know. Who is to say a stranger is not an angel or saint in disguise?

Will you now agree with these words, or deny the existence of an eternal oneness, which is also as diverse as the billions of galaxies and different forms of life throughout creation? Truly, love and light are simple, and are simply everything. May you find the beauty within it, because I will always accept your frailties, strengths and also your weakness too. Finally, today, I ask whether you can you accept each other' and more importantly, can you accept your own? Amen.

LESSON 31:

DENIAL

There will be times when the pull of your heartstrings becomes too great to ignore, and even though each one of you allow the days or weeks to expand before becoming 'still', you are always ready to bathe in the essence of your own divinity.

Strange as it may seem, I do not force these periods upon you, except by your own choices and decisions you make during waking hours. I clearly understand the need to find a balance in your life because of the way you live. That said, with one's family, work, and home responsibilities, many people feel detached from the reality and love inside their hearts.

One could call this bizarre and rather odd, or go as far as saying that when one focuses on the impermanent or the material world, you are just in denial. As you are your own judge and jury, it is for everyone—as an individual spark from my heart of love and light—to decide such things ... after all, no one else can know how happy they think you are at this time.

In its harshest form, to deny me is actually denying 'yourself' and vice versa, but when you are still, true peace and bliss both befalls and radiates from and through and to you. This is not the same as—or to be found upon —sun kissed beaches, mountaintops or colourful fields and valleys of flora. These moments only try to bring me to your attention, as your senses soon fill with the beauty and glory of the same divinity, which is purely a reflection of your true self 'within'.

However, the way most people currently live their lives is one of the exterior. They place a greater importance upon the body, the garments it is clothed in, and all the while imposing self-criticism and anxiety, generated from another's looks, words, or condemning silence.

You are each what you are, so whether one is fat, short, tall, or thin ... these different traits and characteristics do not make one closer or any further away from my heart. So, too, being black, white, yellow or red does not make one more loving, or more prone to the ugliness of a fight. Anger, hate, jealousy and ego and many other negative elements of the 'self' are not dependent upon such things.

Do I love those who are born with so-called deficiencies any less than every else? No! The crucial thing is that the person—or even those who are close to them—do not either. Please understand, when seen with the eyes of truth, you are all complete. How could you not be? Again, this is only another form of denial.

On the 'earth-plane', many countries and nations live in fear from suppressive regimes, dictators, or tyrants, but realise these times are now ending. "Why and how" you might ask? Well, it is through love, compassion, and a desire to feel 'free' by which democracy prevails. People will no longer tolerate such suppression, and therefore there has been a continued uprising of frustration towards heads of state and governments around the world.

You must appreciate, though, violence and hatred have never been the way forward, or the solution to global problems. The responsibility lies with those deemed to be in 'power', to work in kindness with their neighbours, for the welfare and safety of its people. The citizens of each country and continent must share in the obligation to act in non-violence, good conduct, righteousness, truth, peace, and love. Conflict only occurs when either—or both—become fixated on enforcing their own will upon the other.

Closer to your heart, many souls counteract their emotions with denial, anxiety, and fear. In fact, each person will deny themselves countless times in their lives. One of the most severe forms is speaking, but not actually saying what is on your minds. Worse still, is not acting what you speak.

One could state they do not wish to hurt another, but pretending to live in truth brings turmoil to their hearts. Love cannot flow smoothly and effortlessly through one's heart like this, and therefore the body manifests illness, the very symptoms of stress and dis-'ease'.

I must make it clear, you should not just ride roughshod over another's emotions, but there is always an answer to every so-called earthly problem or situation. One cannot find these solutions in the excess of alcohol, drugs, violence, or acts of intimidation through any words or deeds, for true love flows naturally and freely, without coercion. It forgives and accepts what you believe are faults or mistakes.

Know this too, when the heart eases another's pain, colours radiate in spirals of energy, touching others inside and out. Also, when hands are joined, sparks of light emanate like rainbows, arching high and low, and the divine essence reaches way beyond the shore where you reside. You are each a link in one united chain of love, and all beings and souls are 'hallmarked' with truth, which is embedded deep within.

Remember, I do not measure your worth in terms of carats or weight, because you are all highly prized and cherished. Your sparkle and effluence can shine through your character and personalities, reflecting like multi-faceted diamonds, or can turn out dull and tarnished like soft gold, which becomes scratched, picked and worn away by increasing levels of darkness and decay.

Also, throughout your working life, I often see you strive for bigger, better thing. Some people become fixated and attached to the impermanent things of this world. I do not say you can or cannot get these, but state one should take them at face value for what they are.

Such items and sensory pleasures are but trinkets, which are left behind when your current sojourn—soul-journey—ends. Therefore, your legacy is the good you do, the help you give to all those near and far, and the love you freely share and give to all life upon the 'earth-plane' and beyond, within the realms of light and vibration.

No one can deny these facts, because you would just be denying yourself … and therefore me, too. Each life journey can then be amazing, no matter where or when your physical embodiment appears. Some may experience more pain than joy, and others will become disillusioned with their lot, but in whatever circumstances or role you play, know this stage of life can be a platform to achieve immense and wonderful things.

So, like an actor on a stage or in a film, what type of recital will you provide? Do you think you can display your talents only once? Can you shine each day with a theatre performance, night after night, through determination, perseverance, fortitude, and goodwill for the world to experience and share?

Understand too, just like a show, there will be intervals of respite, nourishment, and times to reflect upon the why, what, and how you interact with the audience who meet you every day. In contrast, there are bound to be moments when you struggle, or think you are not giving your best, but it is beyond those you can present your true worth.

Within you is the destiny to rise above so-called negative situations and circumstances which attempt to drag you under the mire of confusion. You can perceive every day as just being another test to overcome, or an opportunity to show the latent gifts bestowed upon—and inside—you.

I can and will 'work' through you all; but you just need to let me, so command and ask me to direct you to the correct scene and a chance to express the light and love inside you. Remember my promise, though, that even when no one is observing or watching, you cannot keep any secret from me. One can act with no cares in the world, or with care and responsibility for each other—and the world.

By living in truth, you may not seem to get the plaudits, accolades or standing ovations, but know your soul will shine eternally beyond those imitation lights, which fade away when popularity wanes, or as the gratitude and opportunities cease. Within my heart, comprehend your spark of divinity will always and forever stay a brilliance of a thousand or even a billion suns. Amen.

LESSON 32:

DREAMING

It is quite clear that many of you are still unsure of what is real and what illusion and confusion really are. We can relate this to living within a daydream, or moreover, a nightmare, which leads to anxiety, uncertainty, and a longing for an escape from countless fears.

While you walk upon the Earth, some believe they have it all … where they live a life full of luxury, where everything can be bought. For others, it can simply be an overwhelming joy and the realization of a roof over their heads, clothes on their backs, and food and water to consume. So, are human beings destined to always see this division between rich and poor, and the different colours and creeds of man? The answer, of course, is no.

Therefore, it is important to understand the mind and how it tries to manipulate and bend both thought and desire. Some call it the 'monkey' mind for obvious reasons, because it takes effort to control, especially when your senses can be manipulated, persuaded, and directed away from one's heart and the truth.

Indeed, the eyes often see the worst of things. Your ears may hear Chinese whispers. Your tongue frequently speaks untruths … and your hands try to influence or bend to a false will, and instead of the sweet fragrance of love … the atmosphere can be drenched with the fear of the unknown.

So, how can you change or deflect the impostors of one's fake character and personality? Well, you could start by becoming like your dreams of deep sleep, for within them, you can be 'free' to be yourself, experiencing joy, friendship, and love. Do not be confused, though. You are all already free in the true sense of the word, as man-made walls and fences can never contain your heart, or by becoming imprisoned by dictators, captors, or any evil regime.

This is a fact, as distance or time can not weaken love as it transcends both, cutting through them more easily than a knife in butter. In addition, it expands and remains beyond the veil of bodily death, and does not fade like fleeting memories, or the dreams in those levels of the subconscious where the mind clings on, and with its demise, attempts to regulate your thoughts and deeds. No, I am talking about those so-called 'Godly' or divine interactions, which I provide for you.

Simply put, most of what occurs during sleep state relates to your feelings and actions in your daily lives, with those stresses and strains influencing to, through and from the mind and its following interpretations. However, when you need the truth and spiritual guidance, you will sense the difference. Some are quite subtle, which show a different—and more refined—frequency and resonance.

Afterwards, your energy spirals through the chakras of your mental, emotional, and physical body, which radiates through to your higher self. These, filter through the ether, to where my love flows like water over rock … cleansing and clearing the murky depths of your consciousness.

Here you sense and experience 'me' as free as a bird, floating through and upon the thermals in the sky … and fly with ease both far and wide, across the 'earth-plane' or beyond. These dreams you receive from the heart are more colourful and profound and can help you because of the information they contain. Remember, no two are alike—even if they seem to be—just as two flowers of the same variety can never be exact in the size of their petals or stem.

They can provide you with the clues and insight you require. Then, sometimes when you wake, this realization can resemble finding the missing piece of the jigsaw puzzle, enabling you to see the whole picture … or rather more, you become a witness to your own truth.

People often want an easier route or explanation, and state, "Why don't you just tell us how to solve our problems?" Please appreciate, your lives are the continuous result of your own actions—whether past, present, or future—and they contain your own lessons to grow and understand.

Imagine you are now in a school classroom. How much would you learn if the answer were already on the blackboard? Therefore, be strong, in the knowledge I will never leave you. How can you be alone if I live within your heart and you in mine?

I would like you to think about something else for a moment, as if you could make a wish for the future. Is it an earthly desire … perhaps to be rich, live with less stress, be healthier, or even become famous? Instead, could you place your trust in your true self and me, taking each of your days, months, and years ahead in the understanding that through faith and love I am with you, releasing those false fears, which the mind attempts to trap you with? Believe me, for I know what you need, rather than what you think you want or desire.

Sometimes it will help you if you become more childlike, too. Not through being irresponsible, mischievous, or overly needy, but being more inquisitive, selfless, and carefree. These attributes can easily be attained with contentment, and a greater understanding of your fellow man—and nature—too.

Another aspect of your daily lives is where your mind is constantly searching, wavering, or daydreaming. Do you focus upon the activity or job in hand, or do you find your attention drifting, momentarily basking in those desires, to be dropped like coins into wishing wells of hope?

Please understand, I never drain your aspirations or concerns from hearts of truth and love, as it is impossible for me to do so as we are 'one'. This is why I know every single being and soul throughout all time and energy and dimension. I do not need or want anything, other than to guide you in your efforts to understand the self-realization of your own divinity—which will enable you to find your true purpose and existence, away from this false desire for any dream world(s).

Likewise, if you have been—or are—currently 'in love', you know its power and essence cannot be quantified. Some feel they cannot sleep or concentrate until another's heart has joined their own, while stomachs keep turning with a constant longing to be together. This feeling is true and pure. Any so-called 'faults' are dismissed, and contentment fulfils each moment as one, not two. Happiness prevails because there is no coercion and manipulation. Iis not forced or made by anyone else's hand.

In reality, our love is even more unique. It is permanent, and does not fade, unlike two hearts which can fall out of love … perhaps through complacency or a lack of tolerance, and mind control over bodily senses. Indeed, the essence I speak of is no illusion, and is found when man rises above the body's consciousness … to live from and through and to the heart.

Even so, I fully appreciate the paths you each take, and the whys, what's and the wherefores, but realize the same power is within every life to help make dreams come true. Remember, I can lift the broken in will or Spirit. Why should any soul have to dream of a single meal or a glass of water to quench their thirst? Or shed tears to have a friend, or become desperate to find shelter and live without fear and pain … or even wish they were somewhere or someone else?

Comprehend that what any man believes as imperfection cannot be, for you are all perfect within my heart. Characters and personalities can contain many flaws which affect others, but the divine flame and spark still resides inside you all, however illumined or obscured it may be.

Therefore, by living in truth and by joining hands of love and light with your neighbour, the world can shine infinitely brighter. All it takes is the contentment and perseverance of—and for—each soul. Know that bridges can be built; and mountains can be moved in the name of peace.

So, ask yourself today, is this a fantasy? If it is, find the strength within to make it a reality. You all have the will and the power to unite under the banner of love and shine together into eternity. The mind may say no, while the heart says yes ... so learn where the real dream starts, and false ones stop. Fulfil now your destiny ... world without end. Amen.

LESSON 33:

INSPIRATION

Around the world, and upon many planets in countless galaxies, a greater number of souls can now recall the truth. Some may hear me; others will see me, and even more feel my love inside their hearts to 'know' me. In fact, the further you strive towards me, brings a heightened sense and awareness of my presence—be this on the Earth, in the sky, or floating upon or within any stream, river, lake, or sea.

Of course, throughout history and time, people believed—or instinctively knew—something far greater than themselves exists. In their searching and yearning they looked beyond imaginary boundaries and even the stars to find a so-called 'heaven' or God … all because they could see, not only through earthly eyes, but also with their heart and mind and soul to know the true 'I'.

While someone's religious beliefs remain strong, the mystery of me should be easier to comprehend, as faith brings trust. If you trust, you can believe with all your heart. Remember, I do not hide from anyone of you, for 'I am I' in all places and everything … so you can sense that I am right beside, in front, behind, above, below and within you.

Therefore, if you accept this as reality, where else can I be? And if so, please realise I am always with you, and hence I observe the constant rush to achieve your daily tasks. You resemble a whirlwind—spiralling back and forth—with no true direction or purpose. Indeed, the mind will seem engaged, or enraged, with countless decisions and choices to be made. One may even think I imply less effort is being made regarding one's duties of work, home, or family responsibilities, but in fact I aim to highlight golden opportunities which are being overlooked by many a heart and soul.

Within every life, I constantly leave you clues and messages. Some are subliminal—while others glare you right in your face—and yet they can still be missed! I might send you the right song to hear on the radio, or you even overhear a conversation which triggers a memory or feeling.

What about a fragrance, too, which reminds you of someone or something personal? Perhaps you will gaze upon a beautiful sunset, or bear witness to an incredible picture or photograph? Or … you simply hug and kiss your beloved husband, wife, daughter, son or pet, triggering both joy and comfort deep inside you.

These are a few examples of how I connect with your own divine spark and essence. With this connection, not only do you start to imagine you are 'complete', but you also become inspired to think about and search for answers in your soul too.

Understand it is here and here alone where beautiful colours reign, for true love is not found by separating the black and white, or the dark and light. Remember, it is you who captured me. I am contained not through coercion, as I am the lock … you are the key, and your heart is already free.

Therefore, no other combination is required or has to be remembered. It does not matter what number of souls or beings are sown and scattered throughout creation; we are all 'one'. Try to see all life as being part of you, and equal, too. No more—or any less—special than yourself. Are not the cats, dogs, rodents, insects, birds, bees, or any other creature worthy of my love too?

Likewise, if you imagined I was a tree, and the fruit upon my branches are souls, do those growing in the shade have less vitality? Shouldn't those who grow on my lower limbs deserve my love too? You are all precisely where you are meant to be, as there is a purpose and reason—both karmic and/or otherwise—to be 'whom' and what you are.

Do not be confused or intimidated through the mind's false deception, inciting any twists of fate or bad luck. Comprehend, cause and effect and a balance between hearts and any precious 'soul-journeys', remain true for everyone. So, the purpose of living is for love, which can last for just a few moments or become decades of your Earth years … whereas your goal is self-realization, which leads to bliss and peace.

I cannot provide you with a magic formula to digest or inhale. Likewise, no change in your bodily overcoat can disguise the effluence or the lightness and brilliance of your own divinity to me. What I will always deliver—to you—are the opportunities and incidents which arrive precisely when they are meant to You just have to be aware of them.

I promise to give you the inspiration, though, to nudge your heart in the right direction. Then you will know you are walking upon the pathway of truth, because it will feel inherently different to how you did before. Deep inside, you are now the round peg fitting neatly into the round hole. No matter when or where this occurs, it is for you to believe, as what is right for one may not resonate with another.

Indeed, your own truth fits you like your favourite pair of shoes, but deceit, anger and hate are like wearing those which are two sizes too small. Similarly, if or when you become confused, to stop and test me—and yourself—the footwear worn on the path you take will appear two sizes too big. This will give you no balance at all, slipping and sliding, taking two steps forward and one-step back.

In time, doors open, and they create opportunities for every one of you. When something is right, it is like the sun suddenly breaking free from rain-filled clouds or rising above the dark horizon. Try not to despair, fear or ask about the timing of such things, even though I know what you need before you have ever thought of it.

Realise that within your heart lies the magnificent power of love and light. It knows no bounds and is without limitation or restriction. Therefore, you can each achieve great and glorious things to help yourself and fellow hearts and souls upon the 'earth-plane', and far beyond it, too.

Please appreciate, these choices are yours alone to make, and no one can live your life for you. It is your own soul's responsibility. Understand too, by your awareness and strength within you, your personality and character can shine, and this helps to maintain your bodily health, which enables you to achieve your own goals and ambitions.

You may well experience both sorrow and pain, along with tears of laughter in your life. In addition, try not to be excitable at fleeting pleasures or praise, or become deflated by criticism from another's so-called faults or ego. Please look for the goodness inside you, and in others, too. At the same time, find the inspiration through your creativity and those gifts bestowed upon you. Perhaps you can discover your passion, and, if you can follow this, who knows what you can achieve ... you might surprise yourself!

Do not be overly concerned with the fruits of your labour—which is easier said than done in the age in which you currently live. In whatever you do and wherever you go, just believe in yourself and be the best you can be in order to serve and help others. Remember, you always receive what you need.

Overall, anyone of you can become inspired, and even find inspiration in another person. Perhaps a famous film star or celebrity? This is fine ... if you then find your true pathway we spoke of earlier. However, your own motivation is always within you, and it is waiting, hoping, and wishing for you to find it.

Therefore, open your heart and go deep inside to sense the illumination of your inner child—for your divinity is willing you to shine more radiantly every day. Reveal it. Bask in it and make your dreams a reality ... because I am with you forever. Never doubt this. I love you eternally. So be true, and just be you! Amen.

LESSON 34:

THE WELL

Once again, welcome to thy speaking heart! Please understand, I now wish you to bathe in the well of your own divine essence … because so many of your waking hours are consumed with family, home, and work responsibilities, which become used without true thought. Minute-by-minute, hour-by-hour and day-by-day the clock drifts by, so you state, "Where did that day, week, month or year go?" Well, upon the earthly vibration and world, time is a constant reminder that it waits for no one, but is still a gift I pre-sent to every one of you.

What you do with such a precious commodity is entirely your own decision, but this can help you remember to live in the world, but not be attached to it. Do not be perplexed, confused, annoyed or even frustrated by 'words'. You can shine and share your love and remain unattached to the desires—from the senses—for the impermanent world where you currently live.

This does not mean these traits and acts of compassion, forgiveness, and kindness should ever be forgotten. In fact, they ought to become commonplace, noticeable by all hearts and minds, no matter one's colour, creed, nationality, or religion. These will leave reminders of experience, not only as lines etched upon the face over many decades, but also within the soul. You can then draw on such memories throughout your life, lifting the bucket of emotions from the well of your heart, which is deep inside you—and where I no longer seem hidden—so please quench your thirst for truth and love.

Like the water wells from days of old, it takes physical effort to raise the natural resources so freely given by Mother-Earth. Without water, your body would die, but what about your divinity? What do you think sustains its illumination and brilliance? Understand, there is only one answer, dear child … 'love'.

Please realise, to travel great distances over land and sea or through the sky to find your true sustenance is not required. Understand, this is of far greater importance to you than air, water, and food. Without love, the soul cannot function … your spark of light and divine essence becomes dull and impoverished. However, each moment can be grasped with eagerness, contentment, and gratitude, as love within your heart and soul—and through trust and faith—does not thrive upon separation and illusion, but seeks the truth, and only this reality quenches thy inner thirst.

So, if you were to pull the bucket up from a water well, it may be full, half-full, or even empty. Appreciate the well of my heart will never run dry. If you truly wish to seek and desire me, I will always fulfil you. This is not a contract or a verbal agreement, because you are responsible for your own thoughts, words, actions, and deeds.

I say these things to explain I am forever here, there, and everywhere for you all, so it is down to the so-called 'individual' whether he or she will search and aspire to understand and know me within. Likewise, by accepting yourself, you will surely accept me too, for I am you and you are me, as we are one, remember!

Therefore, with each passing day, choices and decisions rise like the sun. When you look for them, they become clearer and resemble sunlight shining through clouds of confusion, which helps to clear dense fog from the mind. This is important, for when agitated—through so many negative traits like anger, jealousy, hatred, and ego—the way forward becomes blurred and hazy. It is like viewing a mirage, believing something or someone is there, and this leads to false hope, denial, and pain.

By becoming focused and true within, you endeavour to better oneself on a soul level. The doors will open, and opportunities materialize, which enables you to shine and share from and to and through the heart. These will leave lasting impressions on other souls, not like those memories which resemble ripples, fading on the emotional waters of life. Therefore, with each new day that dawns, can you arise with vigour and anticipation ... or do you glance back upon the imprint of your slumber, where time does not separate those sleep or waking hours?

Please know, there is so much the individual—and the masses—can achieve if you only believe in yourselves. By linking those chains of love, which I previously discussed, then the truest connection of all can be realised ... your eternal goal of bliss and peace within me.

Appreciate too, your current embodiment and 'sojourns' are temporary elements, so do not think of these months and years as something perpetual. In reality, they are but a click of a finger ... as I have described to you many times before. Even so, time can be as valuable as you each make it to be. Like the blank canvass in front of an artist, your character and personality will depict the image being portrayed for others to see.

Remember, I do not favour rich or poor, tall or small, fat or thin, so let the colours of truth and love and light be the pallet of one's heart, which brings your own soul's picture to life. As you move forward, you may make unclear choices ... and what you believe are mistakes. Some of your decisions are the reasons those images merge and blend. They reflect those moments when friendships become strained and the subsequent tension cause voices to be raised, attempting to overrule what seems another's incorrect thoughts and actions.

Once again though, by drawing from the well of love, so much can be overcome ... and even more can be revealed and displayed. Imagine you were painting by numbers. You will soon realise you are being guided and directed to not only the right colour but also your emotions, then portray the picture of truth for all to see.

Upon completion, your life—just like a photograph—will have captured a snapshot containing your soul's memory and experience, with my grace as the frame that displays, holds, and protects you in a loving embrace. So, how much effort will you now put into your day, and will you let the canvass remain the same? What changes can you make too, both within and without yourself, to reveal the true you? Are you able to mix the true colours of your smile and a hand of friendship with the divinity which adoringly flows so freely to you?

Would you also deny the opportunity for another's heart to see yours, because you cannot move the once free flowing brush which is now clogged up? Has the pallet of loving oil been sadly mixed with lower based emotions? Indeed, water and oil do not mix and rightly so. But like the light and dark, they often wish to be expressed. In fact, one cannot exist without the other.

Overall, it is you and only you who can determine your own legacy ... yet to be revealed. Therefore, may the picture you create be the reminder of your soul that adorns the memories of many hearts. If you can but find the divine essence of 'I' inside you, your passion, creativity, energy, and life's purpose will flow like a waterfall of my eternal tears ... which will guide, encourage, uplift, and love you forever more. Amen.

LESSON 35:

HEART TO HEART

Welcome to all hearts and souls. Once again, one may ponder over the minutes, hours, days, weeks, months, and years as they fly by … not unlike those passing clouds, which soon fade past your window. There will be times like this throughout your life, when you wonder where you're headed, and for what purpose, too.

In fact, all such questions form in the recesses of your mind. They then drip into the pool of your consciousness, before turning into waves of discontent … and all because your queries about who, what and why you exist become even closer to each other, bringing greater worry or fear.

Remember though, if you go with the flow, these will soon turn to ripples, which change into smoother waters. This brings balance, peace, and tranquillity to the shores where your heart and physical being live. In all walks of life, you must believe in yourself. When you do, your faith in me will grow, too. After all, if you cannot trust in the true wave, how can you trust the one ocean?

Try to understand, if you think you do not know whether you are coming or going, it is the 'push me-pull you' effect being transferred from the ether into the physical world, but all circumstances are for an individual's growth, even if one does not identify or know this at the time.

Events, situations, and strange happenings can seem sporadic, ad hoc, or misshapen, but this is never the case. How complex do you think life has to be in order to ensure the right conditions occur precisely when they are meant to for every soul? One cannot even contemplate the logic behind this yet, but appreciate love knows no bounds, and is all power and energy, so this is a start.

Through uncertainty and confusion across the world, many will see nations in conflict with their citizens, while war, famine and disease all lead to an uncertain future. Please realise here, it is not I who is unsure about anyone or anything—and neither should you be—because ultimately, there is no greater power than love.

In such periods, it is quite easy to feel affected by incidents which prompt an outpouring of emotions. This may trigger donations of time, money, and assets from one person, one country, or one nation to another. So you can accomplish much when hands are genuinely linked with your neighbour. However, as time passes, headline news, as well as thoughts and feelings change, so it's much easier to forget emotions of the past, but it is important true memories within the heart do not.

Therefore, how can one stay focused? What should one do to keep to the truth? Well, why not sit with me and have a 'heart to heart'. When one speaks to the other, love is transmitted. So, if there are 1,440 minutes in your day, how many are used where you sense and share in our connection of love and light?

Perhaps you could try to be still, and in effect, take another step closer by being conscious of me inside your heart. We can laugh, sing, and cry with tears of sadness and joy together; you only need to call on me … though I am already with you before you even think or speak.

Upon the 'earth-plane', if you become unsure of something, or wish to share intimate thoughts with someone, you could also describe these times as having a 'heart to heart'. In essence, are we not doing the same thing? In fact, most people only seem to connect with each other during moments of strong—or painful—experiences, for it becomes a reality while you are emotional.

Can two people become closer when their hearts are aching, even if the cause is through illness or a so-called 'tragedy' … either personal or global? If you're unsure, please try to understand, if truth pierces a heart, it can still bleed with—or for—compassion, hope and faith.

Remember, when you are still, boundless peace and bliss envelops your mental, physical, and spiritual/ethereal bodies. By experiencing this—as love encompasses you—tears may fall upon your face. But inside the chambers of your heart, they crystallize and shine forth from your soul, which reflects your effervescence and brilliance like a star. It is here I see your divinity revealed, for no secrets can ever lie hidden.

I state these things, only to explain that after your love is expressed, you always feel better. In all circumstances, one will constantly become 'lighter'—as if it has removed a lead weight from your shoulders. Indeed, it has been, for I take your burdens upon myself. Some may question why I do this. It is because I am your friend, confidant, guardian, mother, father, and am all things, and I will never leave you, for we are inseparable.

As I witness many of your days drifting by … thinking, toiling, and in worry from morning through to the evening, time is indeed ticking by without contemplation of your own reality within. Therefore, by refocusing upon the inner joy of being you, you will understand it is I who am the 'doer', not yourself as the body and mind.

By re-inviting me into your life, I can shine through all the abilities and senses you possess. Hence your actions, then bear fruit for other's seeking sustenance and growth. The milk of human kindness will pour from person to person, city to city, and nation to nation. The world only needs to believe and act in truth for this to become real.

Wherever you are, you may indeed seem small, insignificant, or even dispensable, but you are not. Like an ingredient missing from a meal, it would not go unnoticed. If a take a single cog from an old clock, its hands would fail to turn. Likewise, a torch will fade and disappear without all the battery cells within it. Comprehend, there is no difference with each soul … which is why the Earth and humanity need everyone to connect and illuminate in these current times. Can you help each other, and in doing so, aid yourself? Will you link in unison, or be as negative and positive … seemingly poles apart?

Please try to let your love flow from, through and to you always, in all ways. Opportunities will present themselves in every aspect of your existence, within your home, family, work, and social lives, too. Each one can be used and shared for truth and honesty, without prejudice, and with sincerity. In essence, they resemble butterflies' wings, which silently beat upon the breeze, and yet they carry echoes of peace and kindness to resonate over mountains of ego and pain, captured over countless lifetimes.

Know that my love will melt the ice, which has been frozen around those hearts held captive by fear, darkness, and decay. Like the sun, it shall beam and radiate new light, growth, and understanding deep inside you. Then, you enlighten others in new directions because we are all 'one'. Upon this day, if you cannot be 'still' and sit within the seat of your soul, why not speak to a friend, and have a good old heart to heart instead? Amen.

LESSON 36:

RUINS

May each heart bear witness to these words, whether read in your mind, spoken out loud, or even shouted from the rooftops! And perhaps they can become etched deep inside you, because throughout Earth's history—and in fact since time immemorial—all impermanent things rot, crumble, and fall into decay. There are no preservatives known to man that will stabilize wood, steel, stone, flesh, or bone into eternity.

Indeed, one may even currently believe the molecules, DNA, microbes, and the like can be frozen in time, but this is not a constant which forgives or succumbs to such notions. Why? Well, it is because life is not one, two or even three-dimensional. The core essence of the soul, once it has left its denser bodily structure, removes the life force and energy which sustained it. All the remaining elements will eventually perish ... even if it takes many hundreds, thousands, or even millions of years.

The reasons I highlight these facts are twofold. First, to make you think about your own mortality. Second, for you to consider the important aspects of your life. In doing so, one can reflect upon what truly stands the test of time and of your eternal legacy.

As stated, many times before, each day you breathe is a gift. However, what you do with it is entirely up to you. Remember though, whether you believe you are alone, or if you are keeping company amongst thousands of people, your thoughts can help others and can carry the energy of love without boundaries or limitations.

One should note, when these are given freely, sincerely, and wantonly, they are most powerful. They shine and rise like a phoenix from the ashes. In contrast, any vibration of anger or hatred and fear tries to destroy the very fabric of structure and order, and one's own self-control may waver.

In the worst scenario, the body would resemble a vehicle grinding to a halt without the oil needed to lubricate vital parts of the engine. One might compare this as being devoid of love. In truth, one has simply ceased to pay attention to one's own body and your heart's and soul's requirements. Comprehend this, 'man' cannot exist without love. It transmutes and encompasses all religions and faiths, every colour, creed, and all life.

Therefore, your own divinity requires devotion, like cultivating a flowerbed. If left unkempt and unattended, it is easy for weeds to bind and suffocate the plants and flowers. Likewise, your divine essence and fragrance will not rise from the plumes and petals of your heart. They become stifled and trapped, thus requiring even greater persistence to remove the negative cause-and-effect scenario. You can achieve this from a helping hand, or by one's own grit and determination. Then, by focusing upon me, you will feel immeasurable power, love, and guidance, but can you —or do you even want to—believe this?

Throughout 'history', countless relics—from many eras—are unearthed. Each tell their individual story. These are links to someone or something's past; and can reveal the way they lived, or even how they were physically 'formed', and then come to pass. Scientists, archaeologists, and historians map precise locations, and with carbon dating, attempt to connect theory with reason, no matter what the season. They endeavour to understand the why, what, and wherefore, to build accurate pictures and assess the turn of events.

In contrast, each of you must grasp the circumstances and situations which unfold in your own lives too, be it on a daily, weekly, monthly, or yearly basis, for they materialize like signposts upon your soul's journey in this lifetime. Every thought, word and deed can resemble crumbs of self-comfort and even pity, or they become seeds of truth. You cast them on and through the ether, but which do you follow? Is it the breadcrumbs of 'desire', or those brand-new paths to explore and shine your innermost light and being?

These choices are your own to make, but guidance is forever with you through your intuition, conscience, and from and through and to those who link with you upon the ethereal planes, and of course those on the 'earth-plane' too.

I also urge you to build your inner defence like castle walls, and even if someone feels or believes they are weak in body or mind, please know, in your weakness, I will strengthen you. I understand your body—but even more so your heart—is under a constant barrage of negativity, despair, anguish, and greed.

Like an army of parasites, they nibble away, attempting to break through, causing havoc and pain. They try to trick your mind, weaken your resolve, and make the walls of truth, dignity, love, and compassion tumble down. Ultimately, such foes appear to stem from beyond the barricades of love, because they have already infiltrated the mind during previous moments of weakness. However, by being vigilant and living life with fortitude and perseverance, you can eradicate harmful tendencies and indiscretions.

So, how can you remove them, whilst at the same time hold new threats at bay? Well, you need to rise above trivialities; forgive another's words, actions, and deeds against you. You can ask yourself if what you are saying, doing, planning is detrimental to another and is befitting of you to be called a human being.

I ask you to fulfil your real potential. You are only ever limited ... by your own imagination. By discovering your true self, you will know me. By knowing me, you have self-realization, and through this, discover your own divinity. You will never fear or live in anxiety and misapprehension ever again.

Therefore, appreciate the light is your essence and fortress, and love is all things ... the eternal glue which binds you all to me and me to you. It is permanent and can never descend into ruin. Remember, only what appears in the impermanent world in which your body lives can this seem like this.

When humanity realises it is 'one', all the false defences around nation-to-nation, city-to-city, and those between every heart will fall. These will be the only ruins to be 'celebrated' by all, forever and a day. Amen.

LESSON 37:

SOUNDS AND FEELINGS

Welcome, and rejoice in the peace and tranquillity, for as you sit quietly, your mind becomes less agitated when stillness washes over you. Now, as you become bathed in the autumn sunshine, sunlight streams down to warm your face and body, and I sense such gladness for this moment.

This never ceases to amaze me. You long for this feeling upon your exterior 'self', but often forget the affluence, sustenance, and amazing light inside you. However, to experience this beautiful aspect of living in the impermanent world should never be underestimated, as the Sun gives and maintains life's essence in the world.

Try to put your thoughts on hold for a while. Listen as a strong breeze rattles the branches of the trees nearby. Leaves also rustle inside the borders of the garden, and the occasional melody and birdsong break the silence too ... indeed, you can hear me, as all these things ... 'I AM'.

The fresh air fills your lungs with gratitude, and because you feel 'alive', this brings positive energy, which radiates through all life in such times of stillness and contentment. Suddenly, a grey cloud passes across the Sun, but you can see and sense it is only temporary, as the blue sky soon returns once more, which is a precise reflection of those trials and tribulations within all life.

Remember ... anxiety, worry and fear will forever enter those tasks to complete, as long as you do not rise above shadow and doubt. Time is a major factor in this. Even dark, painful days of so-called loss and bereavement should become easier to bear. Please understand that during such periods, one's memories may fade, but love stays forever with, from, through, and to you.

Swiftly, as if right on cue, a black cloud appears, forcing you to dive for cover, as torrential rain and even hailstones beat down. Then, but a minute later, only the sound of the slight drizzle remains, trickling down the windowpane ... a mirror image of one's own tears when you feel sad, lonely, or afraid. Appreciate you will experience all these elements, and death inevitably follows your birth of the body into a denser realm and dimension.

Afterwards, as if a magic wand is waved, the peace returns. A brilliant clear sky and sunlight soon bathes your being. Insects and butterflies emerge to fly on the breeze, and a robin stands upon a distant twig, shaking its feathers dry before taking flight. You see, even rain is welcome to some, and an opportunity to be cleansed. One's tears are just the same—for more often than not—you will subsequently see more clearly. In fact, the release is an up swell of your emotions pouring from the heart, not unlike those passing black clouds.

During your earthbound days, please overcome arrogance or irritable circumstances or situations, like a fly buzzing around the room and landing upon you. Consider it only a minor inconvenience. Ask yourself, how do you react in such times? Do you let another's habits consume your attention? Could you rise above someone else's traits, accepting them as no more than mirroring your own?

Please try to realise you are all special and live the life you do for a reason. No one can say they are more important than another. Therefore, can you rise from your bed with a purpose each morning? What really drives, inspires, and motivates you? Does this differ in any way from your spouse, partner, or lover?

As billions of souls walk the Earth, perhaps you could consider what truly unites you all too … for it isn't one currency, creed, or a religion, nor is it accents or words from the tongue. Neither is it the colour of one's hair or eyes. Indeed, it is one thing and one thing only, the true language of the heart, which is 'love'.

Can you describe what this feels or sounds like? Well, pierce the heart of any man, woman, child or being and it will bleed just the same. Break it, and the cry of pain—and those tears that fall—are replicated, whether from north, south, east, or west. No amount of money can place a 'band aid' across broken dreams or promises.

Appreciate it is important to respect someone else's feelings without enforcing your own. In addition, by denying your own false desires, you will comprehend you are not alone, for both override your hidden impulses of selfishness, attachments, and illusion.

On the surface, you might not bear witness to this eventuality, but this is only because love and light is—and works—on every level. So, one may benefit spiritually, emotionally, mentally, or physically. Remember, you always receive whatever you require or need the most.

As you contemplate these things, I sense the calmness within and around your heart. Such occasions energize your whole being. When you are in tune with oneself, know it is here and here alone, where this spark of your divinity shines everlasting through the frequency of love.

People often pray to experience and know 'true' love. What do you think this is? One can try to describe it, but to truly grasp this is like someone trying to explain who, what, why, and how I am. The words of the tongue cannot. Sights, sounds and pleasures of the world in which your embodiment lives also attempt to do the same. So, I shall help and provide you with an inkling of such a query.

Only the heart can appreciate and comprehend the truth, for when you fall in love and look into their eyes, no words need to be exchanged. To wipe the tear gently from your child's cheek, your action rises above speech. By giving water to the thirsty—or food to the hungry—one's hands are holier than lips that pray. In every moment throughout your whole life, when you believe you are at peace, bliss, or ecstasy, and witness spectacular natural phenomenon to gasp in awe, all these together are but a fragment of you and me—and love.

Know too, the stars—which appear to only shine at night—produce both sound and energy, but can you say you hear them? Within the air and the ether, particles of life and light swirl and majestically dance, but can you say see them? Someone—or something—across the other side of the globe may also cry out in agony or pain, too, but can you truly feel them?

In fact, all your senses can assist you, but try not to become a slave to them. As I have continually stated, only through your heart can the resonance of truth be known. Everything else becomes distorted by negativity, distrust, fear, and greed. Imagine the sound of fingernails being run down a blackboard, causing you to wince or cringe, compared to the relief when such a noise stops.

I urge you to not only uncover your ears and eyes to the reality and beauty around you, but also block out disturbing waves of the min … which distort your thoughts and connections with your heart. Remember, try to do what you feel and feel what you do. Every day you can rise to the challenge of living and shining far beyond the walls in which you reside.

You do not need to shout out from your home or castle, or any humble abode in which you live, because your actions speak louder than any words you can say. Know that your helping hand can change another's life, but it can also alter your own. In serving others and society, each man, woman, and country can link their hands, minds, and hearts as one true nation of the world.

One day, the sounds and feelings of this frequency of love will resonate into eternity. Therefore, beginning this day, what difference can you make … and will you now start to mend all hearts? Amen.

LESSON 38:

MORNING

Good morning to you! Today's lesson shall follow in a similar vain to 'Sounds and Feelings', and hopefully expand and glorify your soul too. Therefore, as the Sun rises on a beautiful autumn day, your heart must surely feel the same. Tiredness now fades from your body, like those shadows which disappear from your view.

Looking upwards, sunlight glows upon the leaves of the trees, with one half basking in the coming warmth of the day, the other still in the dark—yet to bear witness to the glory of the light. Like a reflection, all life can appear this way; a subtle reminder of many broken hearts, failed dreams and a false hope … all waiting to materialize upon a horizon. This is sad indeed. Those who live in fear, and stay within the dim shade of dusk, must realise truth, love and clarity are but a step forward or only a heartbeat away.

Realise that as you sit in peace, the world around you appears to be awakening. Birds are singing, the crows and rooks arise from their lofty nests, and even a ladybird drifts on the breeze. In this stillness, who could not appreciate such beauty in creation? And now the sky above is clear and blue, save for a few wispy clouds, formed by Mother-Earth and nature herself. In contrast, several planes fly high and far, and they glisten like silver fish shining in the Sun … leaving trails across the ether, but not for very long.

In fact, this is not dissimilar to many lives, for I see those who open up and shine their light from their hearts, only for negativity—often cast by those whom they love—to smother and cover their divine essence. In these circumstances, confidence can wane, and your creativity becomes stifled or even disappears altogether.

To counteract such things—while developing one's own 'self' to be kind —encourage other people to become an expression of the true love and light you all are. So, when opportunities arise, take advantage of them. Overcome doubt and uncertainty by utilizing your strength inside.

Subsequently, should any other soul wish to manipulate or change who you really are and what you can achieve, understand this affects their own karma too. Therefore, always try to act, be, think, say, and respond with love. If you live in truth, then all consequences I shall uphold and take on as my burden.

Now, as you pause and reflect upon these words, you sense the fresh air, which is not always a benefit afforded to everyone in the world at this time. Therefore, why not spare a thought for those who struggle to breathe—perhaps through illness or injury—and who long to feel this way again.

Indeed, it is so easy to take things for granted in life, be it of nature, friendships, health, home, or family. Sometimes, by pausing from daily needs and desires and the constant rush and stress of a day, you could appreciate not only what others do for you, but what also sustains your well-being both within and out.

Some may disagree or think it's weird, but what one calls trials and tribulations can help you to re-focus and prioritize the elements of your life. This could be at work, rest or play, or regarding your home, family and friends, or even strangers. Remember, through all experiences, your knowledge will turn to wisdom. By becoming more mature—and wiser—you'll become stronger ... like a sapling developing into a mighty oak, able to withstand the turbulence of grief or the winds of change.

You can stay grounded, safe, and secure, in the understanding your faith and trust may sometimes waver ... but will not break. At the same time, you are growing and reaching upwards to the light, towards greater frequencies and resonance of my love. Appreciate, therefore, that each morning can be a blessing or even a curse, depending on your perspective and outlook. Every one of you can look for the positive aspects of your new day and those opportunities to shine from inside your soul.

Now though, as the Sun's light and warmth intensify, one is blessed to be basking within its splendour. One always seems so grateful for such times. And yet, you still remark how dull life can become, when temporarily hidden by cloud. When this occurs, why not try to be like the rays of the Sun instead, for even if their presence isn't seen, you know it always shines.

Likewise, your smile may still light up someone's heart. Your outstretched hand can lift the well-being of another from darkness and depression. Your love shall illuminate and bring joy to other souls, having lost their way under the clouds of illusion and confusion within the impermanent world. Please comprehend, you are a Sun and the Son too! Light from my light, and love from my love ... all 'sparks' of divinity, and eternal.

Once again, clear blue-sky envelopes and serenely cradles the golden star. It stands majestic, seemingly alone, but in truth, it is one of countless stars throughout the universe and creation. One day though—millions of years from now—they will all eventually 'die', ceasing to exist in their current state. However, life and energy is only changed, as it becomes manipulated into other forms.

In contrast, your soul and the radiating coil of your heart can never be destroyed. Its affluence may sometimes dim, but the divine essence is permanent and everlasting inside me. Deep within your mind, these words should reinforce the power of who and what you are. If you believe these things are true, then you shall realise beyond any doubt, you have the immense strength, fortitude, and stamina to take control of your life. Your own indecisiveness and ego only set the limits, but by breaking free from the imaginary shackles which tie and hold you down, knowledge and wisdom will flow through and over you.

I stated many times before, you cannot 'step out of the box', because there is no box, other than the one you imagine and falsely self-impose. This is not 'blue-sky' thinking, but the connection and link between our hearts. So, always follow what resonates within you, and if simple words do not, look for your inspiration elsewhere.

Remember, if you sense this inside you, then it must be true for you at that precise moment in time. But do not despair if you ever feel you're not moving fast enough, because this will only bring its own frustrations.

No, just take each morning as it arrives. Know it is new and full of moments to grow, appreciate, and share. The past is gone. Only in the present lies the true foundations for the future. Grasp it with both hands and your heart, so you can make a difference to your own world around you. Then, by linking love and light with neighbours, friends and family, the radiance of truth can envelop the globe, nation to nation, as one.

Please pause for a moment. Watch the autumn leaves slowly spiral to the ground. Colours of red, orange, and golden brown all float and land where they will; curling up as if to rest … but not at journey's end, for their goodness—and essence—will eventually merge into the earth to be reborn.

Bear in mind too, the physical overcoat is just the same, but 'within' you are not. In this lifetime, whether young or old, and no matter what caste, creed, religion, or faith, you all have the same opportunity to transcend and ascend from these 'earth-plane' sojourns. Will you reach for it? Will you take it? Well … such choices are your own.

Like the hymn, 'Morning has broken'—but you, though—can never be. So forget any past regrets and move forward this day with enthusiasm and renewed determination. Be kind to your soul. Live and be worthy of the love you were, are, and forever shall be. Let today's new dawn light the way, in the knowledge I am eternally within, above, below, beside, in front, and behind you, and in all ways … every single day. Amen.

LESSON 39:

COMFORT ZONES

Once again, I welcome all life, love, and light. Now, as you read or hear this lesson, are you sitting comfortably? Indeed, perhaps you are. Unlike some who are without the privilege of a chair—and unable to rest weary bones—while they contemplate these connections to the heart.

It may seem strange to point this out, but if you try to place your own comforts to one side, then you would surely appreciate there are many people struggling without food, water, or shelter, let alone soft furnishings and the like. In fact, for people who experience hard times—please do not consider those who cannot afford the latest gadget or take away meal—life often provides a prompt 'reality' check. On such occasions, one may realise who their true friends are, and think about the important things in their day-to-day lives. Or they may even question their faith, and whether I actually exist.

Remember, I do not chastise or criticize anyone for striving to achieve personal goals at work, rest, or play. Only that you place these into perspective within the grander scheme of things ... and, of course, for your life's journey. Part of the confusion with your own lifestyles is never stopping to assess your past, what you have accomplished, or where you're headed. Please understand, this is because of the mind's constant urgency to complete the task or activity you're engaged in. It then moves on to the next and so on and so forth, but this can only make you restless, irritable, and dissatisfied.

There can be many aspects to being in a comfort zone ... the physical body which I mention above, as well as the emotional and mental elements too. Upon vast levels of vibration and energy, I know every soul who declines the paths which materialize before them. One can consider anxiety, failure, and any potential ridicule, which can be more painful than the sword.

However, it is vital each form of life tries to overcome such thoughts, for if you trust in yourself, then you trust me. I fully appreciate having confidence is not something you can buy on a shelf, "I'll have two jars, packets or bags of that please" ... but realize the power, sustenance, and endurance all live deep inside you. Your so-called problems can become nothing more than speed bumps upon the highroad of your life.

With true endeavour, the cocoon of complacency can be broken. You can break down the self-imposed walls built around you. Likewise, by living a life with truth, honesty, integrity, and determination, you can break through the trepidation and fear of the unknown … one's own illusion and confusion.

Therefore, at what point does one become satisfied with their lot? Can you ever be content? Remember, you cannot impress me by trying to keep up with the 'Jones's'. Do you really need a bigger house or car? Does a millionaire strive for their next million because they want to, or feel they must do?

As explained before, there is nothing wrong with attempting to reach your personal dreams. However, inside your heart, I wish to plant seeds of truth and enable the real reasons to flourish and bloom. Contentment allows you to base decisions and life choices on reality rather than desire, which only tricks the mind—and dulls the senses with greed, jealousy, infatuation, deceit, and lies.

Please do not be mistaken about what I state here. The comforts of living differ from what you sense within yourself. When you are still—bearing witness to the love of you and I—there is no greater comfort zone in existence. Here, your heart comprehends you are one with me, which words cannot truly describe.

Therefore, as you live out your days, months, and years, what do you actually strive and wish for? Is it a hot meal, for friendship, finding work to fulfil ambitions? Perhaps start a family, make a discovery, or what about becoming rich, famous, or even both? It is important to understand that whatever road and path one takes in their life … the clothes you wear, the car you drive, and even the house in which you lay your head down to sleep at night are all side issues.

As discussed frequently before, your true wealth is in your personality and character. No one will remember you for how much money you earned or spent, but many hearts will have eternal memories of your kindness, compassion and forgiveness as your soul makes its way through karma and time.

I witness those who step away from their comfort zones in terms of knowledge and wisdom, to display courage and conviction … coming to the aid of another person or different form of life. I do not mean by the physical alone, but also on multiple levels and dimensions accessed in deep sleep or meditation. Countless good deeds take place upon … and within, the ethereal planes, too.

Therefore, when your heart is open, you can—and will—experience what you think are those connections or serendipity 'moments'. Through contemplation, one can appreciate you are indeed guided, watched over, aided, and abetted more than you could ever hope, dream, or wish for. Remember; come away from the old way of thinking and believing that you are always the 'doer'.

Perhaps, even after you have digested these words in the heart and mind, you may believe life is passing you by. Therefore, has the routine of daily living become a grind? Do you feel there is no escape from the sojourn of the soul … which you yourself have made? If so, please listen to me. There is always a way forward if you can believe, hope, and pray there is.

I will assist you through my light hierarchy, whenever and wherever love needs or demands it, so achieve your own personal goals through perseverance, confidence, and belief. If four walls cannot contain your heart, then you must conclude you are already free. So, what is holding you back?

Do not suppose circumstances dictate to you, because the power of your thoughts—through love—can once again manifest the life you deserve to live. This indeed may involve even greater home comforts, but, moreover, a home of kindness, simplicity, togetherness … and with humility, love, and peace.

Your duty is to become more responsible for what you think and say and do. One can guide or assist another, but inevitably, you are your own judge and jury regarding your conduct and pathway in this lifetime. Should you ever think or ask, "Dear God, how am I doing" the reply you receive resembles the effect following the cause.

Trust in yourself every day because you are strong, motivated, and full of purpose and direction. Even if you think you are weak, believe me, you are not. One's true strength can never lie in the physical stature of the body. It is your passion, creativity, and the truth which reveal it from inside your heart and soul.

Today can be the starting point for you to pick yourself up and dust yourself down. Arise now from the comfort zone of any pride or selfishness, and display the love which shines from, through, and to you without end. Over time, all thoughts and actions will become selfless. By helping any other life form, you make offerings to me. This is the true sacrifice, not of fear, hurt or death, but one placed upon the altar of my heart, to be remembered forever and a day. Amen.

LESSON 40:

REST AND RELAXATION

As each of your day's roll into weeks, months, and years … your body ages. Time seems to evaporate, like water into steam. Indeed, decades may come and go, but if you reflect upon them without equanimity, you will probably feel sad. Even fulfilled dreams and ambitions can become tarnished with frustration, anxiety, or fear.

Please understand, there will be those aches and pains endured by the body, mind, and soul too, because you strive to achieve so much on this journey called 'life'. However, if you can trust from within and actually go with the flow, stress from living in the impermanent world will disappear.

It should be quite clear by now that no one else can live your life for you. Choices are always yours to make. Therefore, when time away from family, home and work responsibilities materializes, how can you use it appropriately? Well, in such moments of 'leisure', appreciate any acts of service—towards and for others—creates new pathways which shine like moonlight, gliding across frozen lakes of emotional waters.

Realise by becoming 'still', you can concentrate upon 'us'—and the connection of our hearts—which strengthens your resolve. It will lift your energy and resonance of life. In fact, through meditation, you can experience true rest and relaxation because it encompasses your whole being. In contrast, holidays, and those moments to put your 'feet up' are only experiences of the exterior world.

These often create unimportant memories, which fade away from the real you. They resemble ocean waves washing away patterns, names or sandcastles made upon the shore. If this wasn't true, can you honestly say you can recall precise details of a vacation, holiday, weekend, or even a film or television program from last month, or even one, five, or ten years ago?

The difference lies internally with the soul. Moments spent sharing, giving, and radiating love mean they're forever etched upon and through and from and to the heart. Any earthly means cannot erase these, either. Only through stillness (when your physical body inactive) does it become more enriched than experiencing a good night's sleep. The mind is helpful here. While disengaged—where possible—it removes the constant barriers erected via the senses, which delay you from the true purpose and direction.

Those who are unfamiliar with training the 'monkey' mind, please try to be 'still', with no thought, even for a few seconds. With practice, elevating above your thoughts should become easier for you. Through dedication and persistence, it will soon achieve longer periods. Without distractions, love can flow and resonate through you, cleansing and uplifting your energy and vibration to higher frequencies. These bring new levels of spiritual education during your current embodiment.

This enables you to grow and move within new circles of people and inside spiritual realms, which therefore enable one's karma to be cleared more quickly and efficiently, first through knowledge, and then experience … leading you to wisdom. Please comprehend, though, that you can only ever learn to the level you have reached.

Consequently, how satisfied are you right now? Do you think there is something more for you? Do you believe you can change for the better in some way, shape or form? And what limits are self-imposed, when you can actually make a difference to your own life and those around you? Appreciate many souls leave lasting legacies for the world, and as you also hold the power of creation 'within', you can too.

Well, the clock is ticking. Second-by-second and minute-by-minute is a constant reminder for one and for all … so can you rally to the call? From this day forth, please overcome your doubts. You are much stronger than you think. Do not despair during periods of grey or shadow, because a smile or a song can turn dark nights into sunny days.

Opportunities throughout your life might seem like a distant horizon, but they are nearer than near, sometimes right in front of you. Therefore, by entrusting your time to my will, and not through trepidation and anxiousness of your own, I can carry you purposefully along.

If you can accept you are no longer the 'doer', then you are offering and dedicating all of your thoughts, words, and deeds unto me. Hence, all resulting consequences become my burden, and do not add to any karmic imbalance you may or may not have.

Okay, so where does this leave us? Well, I shall always love you … so please try to love yourself. Then it becomes much easier to share, care, and love all whom you meet. Do not to look for faults in others either, for they can only reflect who and what you are. Forget different shapes, sizes, colours, or creeds, too. These are immaterial, and only mask and cloak the heart in various guises.

'Within' is where truth lives. This is the source of all souls and beings throughout creation. Like the blood, which oozes from any wound across the world, it is all the same colour, and yet contains the differences resembling character and personality, as you are each a unique and precious spark of divine love.

In the case of your day or week, if there is a spare minute or two, how will you spend them? Will you reminisce over the toils of long hours, or overcome irritations and annoyances to dwell and shine deep inside your heart? Remember, those thoughts and feelings travel far beyond the four walls in which you reside. Positive and negative energy spiral and resonate, connecting or disconnecting your love like a relay switch of truth. So, why stop the flow when you already know?

Please comprehend, you alone are your own judge and jury. Therefore, let your intuition and heart help guide and direct you in these matters. If they become obscured for any reason, then listen to your conscience, for that is 'I', whispering to you in the ether, hoping that you pause and reflect upon the innermost thoughts of your mind.

I wish you well in your own endeavours. And strength too, for the challenges which lie ahead for all humankind. In truth, I state you are never, ever alone, and will always reiterate this to you. Do you have a few moments' spare right now? If so, why not have some rest and relaxation, for 'me, myself, and I'? Amen.

LESSON 41:

TOLERANCE

Welcome to all those who draw closer to me this day, not only to read or hear these words ... but so your hearts may be opened, minds cleansed, and souls strengthened by love and light, which emanate and shine eternally.

As your hours and days roll by, they merge into periods of understanding —or even a continued confusion—as each one of you comes across situations or people who test your patience, and some say even their sanity! These arrive in many forms. Acts and deeds they do ... or do not do. Words being said or unsaid. Gestures seen or unseen. Always be aware of this, because they are part and parcel of everyday life or can occur for far greater reasons.

However, what could these be? Why should you feel threatened, angry, frustrated, or confused with a loved one, a friend, or even a stranger's interaction? In addition, to what level are you prepared—or able—to tolerate those indiscretions, annoyance, anger and/or hatred towards yourself, your family, your home, and the surrounding environment? And, what if the same occurred further afield and on a greater scale, regarding your country of birth, or the world, too?

During such times, blood may boil, tempers flare, and then consequences affect other's way beyond your home and boundary of residence. But what can you do? Count to ten, walk away, forgive, and forget? Appreciate such traits are linked. You will find forgiveness and tolerance go hand in hand ... because when you display acceptance; you exude strength, not only of the mind but also of character and in heart.

If you can understand and comprehend that no one is always right, how can one pretend to know the answer to all things? If this were the case, you would not be in a current physical embodiment. Remember, truth is inside your own heart, for there lies the spark and the essence of me, which is your divinity ... though humankind still cannot describe this yet.

One must acknowledge the conflict within (and upon) the mind and body. It occurs again and again, all because someone feels justified in their actions through hearsay, angst, and fear. We can deem this as 'monkey' mind syndrome, leading to rash decisions, negative words, and ill-thought deeds. These create anguish, resentment, and frustration towards another who is connected to you by circumstance, karma … or so-called 'fate'.

It is all too easy to steamroll in, laying down hardened attitudes that remain clearly marked for others to see or follow. So, I implore you from this day forth to change your perception and try to walk the line of truth. By looking at the bigger picture within any scenario, it becomes easier to move forward, concentrating on love—which guides everyone both internally and externally—and is always at your disposal.

Many think I hide during so-called tough or 'bad' times in their life. They believe I am like a thief in the night, lurking between the shadows. Please, never feel this way; because your joy reflects in me—and is mine too—as is all pain of one's life. Everything is an experience, inevitably linked by karmic debt, and those so-called 'good or bad' deeds you yourself have generated through love and light and darkness.

One must appreciate there can be many triumphs, even from diversity, hurt or even death. Imagine for a moment the mother or father whose child has been murdered. Some—but few—will forgive the perpetrator, knowing that through forgiveness and tolerance, it sets them free within heart and mind. Revenge or hatred do not hold them captive. This would forever pick away at one's wellbeing, and in turn cause stress and disease. Such a display guides countless other souls as they witness immense strength and truth in their thought, words, and deeds. Is this something you could do?

I can discuss countless instances … one may lose a limb or a sense from the body and overcome hardship and fear becoming flag bearers and beacons of light over darkness and diversity. A so-called negative experience can be the catalyst of pure devotion and triumph, not only for those directly affected … but also by loved ones and acquaintances who strive to help and support them too. Would these things happen if the original incident did not even take place?

Please believe me, because you can tolerate a lot more than you think you are capable of. You can try taking one-step back, as far too often one is so close to the situation—or scenario—and you become blinded by imaginary facts. These break away into the ether, inhibiting your focus, like having a splinter pierce your flesh or eye (I).

Would you consider how the other person is feeling and thinking, too? Are they ill—of body or mind—which incapacitates their reasoning and reality? Do not be quick to be the judge and jury. You only need to concern yourself with your own thoughts and actions. So, can you hold your head and heart up high? If so, then why worry, as it all becomes my burden.

Some of you state aloud, "Everything happens for a reason" or "What comes around goes around", and there is truth in such words. However, do not concern yourself with them. Remember, I bear witness and know everything, because I am all of creation.

Please know, the absence of tolerance will often occur because something does not materialize, or someone does not act within the accordance with your own thought process or will. In its deepest sense, this is a lack of maturity, though I do not wish for you to feel chastised or belittled at all. Again, you should never judge another's integrity, because in reality, you are only judging your own … like a mirror's reflection.

Some people can strive through life with so-called thick skins. Both negativity and stress from exterior sources simply bounce off them, unable to penetrate or disturb a focused and well-trained mind and open heart. They can lead by example and may state such occurrences are trivial and non-threatening … maintaining a 'what will be will be' thought process. One can take a lot from attitudes like these.

So, where does this leave you this day? Are you feeling troubled by a telephone call, letter, or meeting? Are you seeing eye to eye (I to I), or are you withholding what is inside, from the love which can cure all doubts, fears, and ills? Let it go … just let it go! Release grudges, animosity, and any pent-up frustration. If you cannot be 'still' and turn deep within, listen to your favourite song, or take a walk in the woods to become bathed in nature. Try to uplift your heart and soul. You will feel differently, I guarantee it.

Realise too, people will often deem life upon the Earth as being a 'short or long' time, but it is but a flicker of a flame or a click of the fingers to me. So, please live with passion, integrity, truth, and with love. By being tolerant of so many occurrences—when it is so easy to lose one's 'self'—can actually change your life.

Therefore, next time the driver cuts you up on a road, or the person pushes into the queue, or someone throws garbage onto the floor, ask yourself, is it a big deal? The car in front may only end up ten seconds ahead of you; a person in the queue (or line) may not receive their desired goods or perhaps better theatre, bus, or train seats. Security cameras may see someone throwing rubbish, and if not, I witness their action through love, truth, and light anyway! Alternatively, you could always let the car overtake, let someone go ahead of you, give someone your seat, or pick the offending item up yourself.

In addition, everyone can make a so-called mistake. Therefore, 'life' has always returned at some point into the impermanent world … to learn or re-learn, in order to grow and reach the goal of bliss and peace. In every thought, word, and deed, your heart either shines brightly or glows dimly. So, it is easy for me to know if they intended them to be true—but carrying unforeseen negative results—or whether they purposefully commit an act which causes hurt and tears of pain.

As such, in all lives of every being and soul, I am tolerant of your endeavours. Please try then, from today, to show more patience to each other and every living thing. Remember, the strength to overcome great adversity lies within you, so let tolerance lead and help you to victory! Amen.

LESSON 42:

LAYERS

May every heart and soul understand, although these words are transmuted by pen onto paper, one's mind often takes flight in all directions. These can cause one's hopes and dreams to spark into life. Or they can fade away through a loss of focus, cohesion, and direction.

Appreciate that true deeds—enacted through the heart—will only come to fruition following truthful thoughts. Even then, they usually materialize only by helping, soothing, guiding, or loving another life or being. Without conviction, love's energy travels no distance at all; and, in fact, becomes unable to break through the many layers of the psyche, prevented through—and by—fear, hesitation, and uncertainty.

Therefore, as one goes through their daily life, such occurrences would resemble a curtain of dense fog, which blinds or confuses both the individual and the masses. This will prevent them from continuing to strive forward in their endeavours—which is an illusion that acts like a false friend—but what exactly do I mean by this?

Well, if you were extremely cold, it would be easy to assume the answer to keeping warm would simply to wear more layers of clothes. This carries consequences. In this scenario, the amount you need is many. So, your ability to move and function properly is severely restricted. Here, a problem is not so much resolved, but just redirected in some other way, shape or form.

Likewise, over many millennia, the karmic imbalance remains for countless souls. Their 'debt' is interlaced and woven into a complex maze of both doubt and fear. To explain this, just try to picture yourself at the centre of this warren. Boundaries tall and wide surround each pathway, which only makes you feel even smaller and insignificant. Now, if you reverse such a thought process—whereby love and help are all around you—you'd appreciate no matter where you are … everything you could ever require is only a heartbeat away. But will you ask for it? Or. will you continue to deny yourself in the knowledge these choices are your own to make?

Comprehend, those who can assist you from the higher realms do so through compassion, faith, and forgiveness. They ask for no reward … other than to desire my grace. (The spiritual planes and dimensions are too numerous to mention here, but they all have their own layers of light to learn and live from, too). No soul will ever know how much my love has helped them until their self-realization and understanding of being 'one'.

In reality, any so-called boundaries can be seen as allies, though initially they can seem insurmountable. One may think there is no quick and easy escape route, and that it is best to keep the 'walls' to one side in order to follow the right road or path in front of you. However, what you really need to do is to accept the problem, obstacle, challenge, or difficulty head on.

At first, this will appear the more difficult choice or task and route. Not so, as what seems the easier method way of keeping such at bay may only bring partial relief, and a temporary solution. It is far better to face up to one's own future experiences with dignity and fortitude.

So, trying to break through those walls of impediment can not only be achieved with your own gifts and attributes—which lie within—but through higher levels of light and energy, using my love, together with your own. You can then pick away and remove the sticky black molasses of negativity and karma surrounding the radiating coil of your heart.

In time, as karmic imbalance is destroyed and removed, it will feel like walking through a gap in those tall boundaries. On the other side, another hedge or boundary line may still exist, only smaller and thinner in comparison. Consequently, like an ever-decreasing circle or ripple upon the sea—caused by a heavy stone, cast out by the weight of your own burdens— your heart will become lighter. Thus, creating a smoother, calmer journey as you make your way forward in this embodiment. You, as the 'wave', will soon be conscious of the fact that separateness is false, and eventually merge and blend with the ocean.

So, you see, with perseverance and courage, breaking through those barriers between or around you become much easier. One day, you realise you were free all along. No prison, maze, or any jungle or wilderness can deny those who desire truth, and who wish to walk into the permanence of my heart.

You may sometimes still believe it is only you—in both body and mind— who organizes, arranges, and enables you to carry on … because ego or pride try to refute me. But by pushing these notions to one side, you comprehend you are me and I am you. The ability and strength I bestow upon you can only be recognized inside your heart. This is where you can fully understand me as both doer and receiver.

Okay, earlier I mentioned my spirit realms and layers of dimension. Well, it is important to grasp how these relate and work inside each other. They are of different densities, each a vibration resonating at diverse speeds and directions. Therefore, when any being or soul acclimatizes and reaches the same frequency, they can 'work' and reside upon, through, within, and from it, too.

Visualise a child entering a lift. The curious side of innocence wishes to elevate and rise to what they believe is the top. Unfortunately, this is not yet possible. The term, 'do not to run before you can walk' is sufficient here. Perhaps they will attempt to open the doors too high. Here the light, the resonance, the rate of vibration and energy are too fast and so bright that it would blind and almost bind them to the spot. One can only receive and work to the level that they have reached, as I have stated many times before.

It is important to note, this does not prevent you from guiding love and thoughts and prayers to anywhere at all, because they cut through and into the ether, like a knife through butter. This is why time and distance are irrelevant when it comes to sending and receiving through and too and from the heart's centre. A true connection can resemble someone answering a telephone call from a loved one, just as they were thinking about them. Only truth and love can work this way, both upon the 'earth-plane' and in all places of existence, even beyond the veil of death.

In contrast, symbolically … the lift I speak of can indeed go down many levels too. There is the same in total, and the phrase 'as above, so below' is a term many understand too. This means it can still reach those hearts and souls who lie deep in shadow. In fact, there are many who have 'fallen', even from heavenly or lofty realms, having lost their way into the darkness.

Comprehend the dark cannot exist without light and vice versa. You can do so much to assist those who are trying to reignite their own spark of divinity. They are those who wander in circles and within many shades of black … confused and dazed by deceit and hate.

Perhaps this day, this hour, and this very minute, you could stop what you are doing, close your eyes and open your heart to send love, healing, compassion, and forgiveness to those less fortunate than yourself. This will assist all who have lost their way … especially those who lie so deep in shadow, they struggle to even find the speck of light shining from the lift door 'inside' my heart.

By sharing your own love towards others, even a faint light can still emit and shine. Just like distant 'cat's eyes' reflecting upon a road … it will lead them once more to the truth, bliss, peace, and everlasting joy. All these souls may appear so deeply covered by layers of despair; they imagine they are forgotten—but not by me.

We are all 'one'. So, can you help this day and night—even while you sleep—or will you forget … keeping your own heart hidden, too? Remember, these choices are always your own. Some might say or reply, "Well, if you are God, why don't you just lift them up in an instant?" I could

… but therein lies your own needs and desires. I do not act as any judge and jury but display and shine the scales of justice within each of your own hearts. All souls must find balance and truth. Only by working through—or with you—can I not become accused of favouritism, or neglect.

Every soul and being—and, in fact, all life—is loved beyond comprehension. Therefore, I guarantee only one eternal outcome will succeed … that the love and light forever live in and to and through and from me. So, live and breathe, and be the truth that is you. In shining brightly, you will help each other through every layer of perpetual love and light and amen to that!

LESSON 43:

SACRIFICE

For many people across the world, a memorable date and time approaches once more. Soon, the eleventh hour on the eleventh day of the eleventh month becomes significant for generations, both past and present. Please understand, it not my intention to make anyone feel sad, frustrated or even unsure of the why, what and the wherefores of those who laid their lives on the line, and in doing so, make the ultimate sacrifice.

Realise too, throughout history and the eras of time, conflicts of both heart and mind have ensued across the globe. Likewise, across and upon many planets, planes of energy, and dimensions, too. Is there a reason for it? Can any one person truly comprehend such things? It is more than likely most of you will find this difficult to do, and therefore it is important these passages of text stick to simple analogies and enable a greater understanding for all. Let's just retrace our steps for a moment.

I appreciate—within your everyday life—you can make compromises and personal sacrifices, often with family, friends, neighbours, employers, and towards strangers. One may also give your own time to support another who is ill, lost, cold, hungry, and thirsty, depressed, suffering pain and anguish through the body, mind, or soul.

Remember, I see everything and all things I am. Therefore, I sense these moments as easily as one who wants to open their eyes in the morning. It is instantaneous and happens without thought or word. Know that deeds from the heart shine like starlight, but only when the action is willingly, wantonly, and purposefully, undertaken.

Of course, the recipient will almost always appreciate the results of the act, but the giver—unless proceeding in truth—will not 'resonate' with such a beautiful vibration and energy. This may not be witnessed by those who live on the 'earth-plane', but is readily seen by the light hierarchy, the elementals, and those residing upon different and higher frequencies, too.

Acts of kindness, when carried out with love, reverberate throughout time. They leave an imprint on hearts and souls. They do not fade like footprints on wet sand, or handprints cast as reminders in clay or cement. No, these will all disappear, even this takes thousands or millions of years, because this is inevitable in the impermanent world.

In these modern times in which you live, your thoughts now focus upon the present wars and conflicts taking place around the world, but not forgetting those who previously fought over the decades and centuries. In fact, many of you carry these concerns. You also worry for those who return injured and scarred—emotionally, physically, and mentally—as well as those souls who left their bodies on land, sea or in the air.

I beg of you to be 'united' in love. Every country, nationality, colour, and creed … but without your attachment to the body. Please know that when you grieve for the 'departed', tears often fall upon your cheeks and lips. There lies the hardest thing which you need to remind yourself of. It might help to recall the following words, "Do not stand beside my grave and weep, for I am not there, I do not sleep", as they resonate in the ether during all such moments of sadness and grief.

Across the world, I bear witness to all religions and faiths. While some people lay symbols and mementoes in gratitude, others (who believe they are left behind) want them to know they are still loved. Crucifixes, poppies, and wreaths are carefully placed upon statues … while memories and tears fall onto hallowed turf, which all display their love from, through, and to me, and countless other hearts too.

Please strive to steer yourself away from what you call painful or 'sad' times. Always rejoice in the heart's memory, for you are each a wave of emotion on the ocean of my love. One day, every soul will float upon calmer waters. Here, the turbulence of loneliness or false separation soon becomes erased forever from your hearts.

Do not despair in striving to establish a meaning of it all. The reality is not in faraway lands to which you cannot reach or find. Nor is it withheld through the eons of time by sacred texts or words, which can no longer be deciphered. There is no secret 'secret'. Love is the only answer. It is the key, the door, the way, and the truth. Nothing more and nothing less. If this were not so, you would not even exist.

During such times when souls gather to 'remember' … comprehend that the resonance and trace of light from those who you think are 'lost', shine through and to and from and below and above you. They are also sparks of divinity and love. Therefore, they sense and know your hearts, too.

So, memories of their embodiment and time together with family, friends, and colleagues are as fresh as dew on grass. Their physical bodies may have withered and faded, just like a rose or flower bud—long since picked from its bed—grown upon Earth and nurtured by both the Sun and 'Son'. However, their fragrance, essence and sweetness lie forever safe in my heart … and therefore remain in yours too.

Strange though it seems, time is a great healer. Those who bear a recent passing may deny this, of course. Is this an initial or a natural cause and effect you wonder? Well, just do not fear. Though your mind and memories can indeed fade, your love cannot. It does not matter how or where or when the garment and overcoat of the soul—which you call the body—becomes erased, whether by burial, flame or by any other means.

Therefore, realise there is so much strength within you. Whatever reason, that you cannot be 'still' to find it … then seek it inside others, because their hearts and arms will cradle you as if they are my very own.

Let me take you back for a moment, to a previous 'lesson' of this book. Remember, I explained that by celebrating one's own birthday, it becomes a constant reminder of your embodiment in the world. Well, I am no 'party pooper', but restate this for two reasons.

First, to help you strive from the notion of being body first and soul second—and to lose this attachment inside your minds. Still, those 'gatherings' bring you together as one—even if they are just family and friends—as this brings goodness and confirms connections of hearts. But try to understand the reason behind this, which needs simplifying.

Second, like a birthday, the date of one's passing can also be seen as an anniversary … one which often carries dread, fear, anguish, or anger. Please refrain from these emotions. Only when the physical passes away can the celebration of a life be truly made because the soul has returned once more to their true resonance of being. Remember, they are not within my peace and bliss because I took—or now keep—them away from you, for all things are part of experience, karma, and the light of all creation.

Likewise, those who 'pass over' are as close to you as you want and need them to be. Time, distance, dimension, and different energy and levels cannot detract from the truth that we are all inseparable and are united for all eternity. Therefore, please be glad for each second with those you love and care for. Those cherished times ring and sing like musical notes floating in the ether … falling upon all hearts, minds, and souls throughout my kingdom. Rejoice in your connection and their love, for this can never be erased.

Such understanding is sacred and just, and a sacrifice made in any capacity is righteous and wonderful to sense and witness. In fact, to give one's life to save another is beyond being golden as it becomes a jewel which adorns my crown … and forever glows eternally within both my heart and theirs as one.

Finally, today, please appreciate and acknowledge what one could call the greatest sacrifice known to man … when Jesus gave up his body. This was to remind you of your own divinity—to help you understand the truth—that it is 'within' that you are the true image of me. Amen.

LESSON 44:

REMEMBRANCE

As you sit within the stillness and peace of our connection, you wonder—and ponder—over the context of this lesson. Do not concern yourself with such feelings or notions.

Therefore, forget body consciousness and those worries or irritations which pick at your mind and try to deviate you from the work at hand. Just trust me. Always trust in your 'self' too. Remember, you are an instrument of my love, and so you can move beyond any selfishness from the senses you possess ... and become selfless.

Please understand, I sense the resonance of your heart, and—because of the country you live in—the many links involved with this 11th of November day. I also bear witness to those thoughts of pain and anguish, which are transformed and relayed through images of red poppies.

This symbolism will not go unnoticed. It transcends from the physical to that of energy and vibration across the world. Now, as you picture thousands of poppies falling from way above you, floating upon a breeze cast by my breath, they resemble the tears which trickle down countless faces. Each one is a memory, a pull of the heartstrings which lies eternal. They leave a trace of our love and connection between you and me, because we are all 'one', with no separation or division.

During this period, these days reignite memories and hearts, making it easier to recall troubled times of anger and conflict around the world. Nation vs. nation, continent vs. continent, man vs. man, and throughout all history, this is revealed through horror and pain.

As I have previously spoken in depth about war and peace, we will not dwell upon it here. Everyone should focus upon the meaning within themselves, to reconsider their emotions, and how this influences their thoughts and words and deeds. In addition, why all people and places should live and tolerate each other, both now and in the future too.

In this current age, there are difficulties between countries and religions and the diverse ideals across the planet. Therein lies the differences between 'man'. Yet inside you all are the overall similarity and truth, which is love ... because within the truth in your hearts, there are no variances, and nothing can detract from this.

Spiritually and physically, you are all one. Therefore, if the heart is pierced, it will bleed. Nationality, colour, or creed bears no effect. Likewise, the memory of pain inside you differs not, no matter where you reside, how old you are, or whether you are in the embodiment of a male or female. So, because of the era in which live, you can still remember the World Wars you call I and II, and of course, the more recent troubles between and over lands you describe as the Falkland Islands, Afghanistan, Iraq, and Syria to name a few.

Indeed, many have fallen. Across generations, expanding over thousands of years, people have been slain in deserts, mountains, upon the water or from the air. In order to understand the pain, you would need to recall many past lives, but this is not a privilege the current 'body' can afford.

Only in the soul can you make the memory and remembrance of these experiences. Therefore, today—and the next few days in particular—lead to your historic Armistice when both horrors of conflict and the light of loved ones will shine more brightly. You are living in the here and now. This is the 'present' I provide for you all.

Consequently, you can not only recall friends, family or distant relatives who fell yesteryear, but also the suffering caused by those battles of bodies and minds right now. Realise love knows no bounds—as I keep reiterating—and so time is irrelevant in these matters.

What is vital to lose is the attachment and incorrect sense—and purpose—of your body. You then remove the assumption you are different or separate from one another and me. Remembrance of your loved one(s) will follow too, because of the need to evolve by finding your goal, which is to know and understand the glory of selflessness, and your own divinity.

I stated before (in the written word); it is easy to forget others and think only of self, and the ego this displays. Simple examples of this are when you view family and friend's photographs, as almost instinctively one looks for (or is mainly interested in) the ones which contain your own image. Another occurs when a relative returns home to the family, perhaps with gifts. Would you solely concern yourself with what you might receive? Can you rejoice in the joy of others opening their own presents? Selfishness must become selflessness at all times.

Throughout your week ahead, the symbolism will play its part in your minds and hearts. Across the globe, millions of souls will look to 'their' God, and a sign of hope for the future. Within this, all faiths and religions look upon a figurehead, symbol, or statue, which attempt to depict me as the divinity, love, and light.

For many in the west, this may be the crucifix, and as simplicity is the key, this represents the embodiment of Jesus, his crucifixion and resurrection. Appreciate, when the 'I'—which is the ego—is cut, it diminishes, and forms a cross. Thus, you then find the strength, conviction, and fortitude to win your own internal and external battles of 'self' and fight for the truth. This will enable you to remember who, what, and why you 'are', so you can elevate and rise to transcend above the 'plane' of Man.

Please do not fear or cry while these conflicts of hearts and minds erupt within or around you, as it is easy to be drawn to such things where anger and confusion can manifest and cloud the reality. In turn, this covers the light, ensuring many souls continue to walk in shadow.

While in grief and pain, this may be difficult to comprehend, but try you must. Remember, even if someone you love is not present, they have not disappeared or faded away. They live forever etched within your heart. This connection cannot—and never will be—erased or destroyed.

Thus, do not wish for one side, one country, or one nation to crush or subdue another. Do not state the way someone else lives is better, more refined—and deemed more correct—than any other. This only leads to renewed tensions, disagreements, anger, and frustration with each other. Rather, the world over, every person should discover the undying strength within themselves. This power can overcome the darkness of hate, pain, and conflict, and through selflessness; you will desire—and then obtain—the remembrance of the divinity of man.

As you become reminded of those injured or fallen, know they are not lying in fields of death, because their light has not been extinguished and never can be. The flame of duty, and the commitment to truth and honesty, lie eternally within them and you all.

Appreciate too, I do not—and cannot—favour east over west, north over south, and vice versa. Love and their own divinity empower every soul. This alone enables peace and hope to prevail, and for light to overcome darkness. However, as all are one, there needs to be a balance, hence the positive and negative, dark, and light, and pain and joy. All are inevitably linked, and they are as much a part of each other as you and me.

So, how will you progress or remember this 'Remembrance' Sunday? And if you wear a poppy, do you question why? Then, when this time is over, will you display your heart with the same gratitude and pride? In fact, can you ever recall the tears of past deeds and endeavours, or shall they fade and become distant memories too?

Therefore, as you now see the fields of poppies before your mind's eye, let each one remind you of the connection to one and all. No soul is lost or forgotten and remains forever in my loving embrace. Whatever nationality or religion, and whether you are white, black, yellow, or red … it does not matter to me.

When all souls unite behind the banner of love, you will all remember and rise above the false veil of death to be reborn into eternal bliss. The poppies and tears which fall can become symbols of everlasting peace, forgiveness, hope and the glory of the light … and the divinity of you all. Amen.

LESSON 45:

ME, MYSELF, AND I

I state you are all my 'family'. So, I welcome all life throughout creation to hear, read, see, and feel my love for each one of you. However, it is essential to realise there are certain areas of the world where people still rise from their beds—and also go to sleep—in darkness. In between, the day is what you each make of it. Therefore, you need to recognize those various aspects of your waking hours, which are being controlled and manipulated by thoughts emanating from the mind. And how they affect both decisions and outcomes of the present and future.

When night or gloom descends, please bring light into your thinking. Let the anxiety, fear, and anguish of what has not come to pass fade from your brow. This will guide you away from desire, confusion, and the illusion, inside and out. Remember, one's mind should not dictate to the heart, but it will try to impose its will through your senses. The key is balance, and by making it less reactive to your feelings, you can become more aware of your soul of what is important in your life.

Throughout most of your day, you are concerned about something ... and if you weren't, you would be worried that you were not worried! Does this sound familiar, as you now contemplate these words? Well, please understand your journey ahead is as complex or simple as one makes it. Any obstacles or hurdles are there for numerous reasons. Not only do they help you pause and reflect, but for one's karma and equilibrium, which assists your growth and experience both inside and out.

Do not wish for easier paths or roads. Except the 'now' and shine as brightly as possible, whatever comes your way. I reiterate, you are never alone, even when you think you are. So by being true to yourself, then you are to 'me'. Without division or separation, you are each part of my 'self', and therefore no secrets can be kept, because the real vision of 'I' witnesses everything.

Many of you now comprehend what day this is. Well, those devotees who follow the teachings of Sai Baba—the Avatar of your current age—who left the mortal body earlier this year know his 'birth' day today is a reminder of true love. Hence, divinity will always blossom into your hearts at the same time too.

In fact, we should welcome each day like this. Each one is a fragment of time to be used and spent in, and through, and to and from love. Therefore, try to act, speak, work, rest, and play in truth … with a passion and purpose to be the best soul and human being you can be.

Yes, there will be times when you think you are weak, when life and everything around you become hard to bear, but please listen to me. There is nothing you cannot overcome when you comprehend, we are 'one'. No one on the 'earth-plane' can evaluate the strength and power within you, because, for man, it is unquantifiable. However, those who live in higher frequencies and realms of other dimensions can perceive it, because they can accept this reality.

Please understand, your light is like many burning suns. Rays and plumes of majestic and colourful energy spiral in every direction. Four walls, or any atmospheric pressure, cannot contain or dampen its true essence from penetrating through distance or time. Even so, negative thoughts, personified by actions of anger, hate, jealousy, and fear, will still attempt to hide, disguise, or interrupt the flow of love. Their effects may appear stronger at first, but know they are only temporary … because of the impermanent world where you currently live.

So, wherever you bear witness to the dawn breaking or sun setting, try not to assume you are watching—and experiencing—the power of dark and light over each other. See them as being in conjunction and whole. There can be no darkness without light, and vice versa. If there was no illumination, or even the stars which shine, how could you tell whether it was night or day?

Similarly, without kindness, compassion, and forgiveness emanating from within your heart, would this mean love does not exist? Realise that even in a so-called wicked character … divine light—no matter how dimmed—still exists deep inside. Remember, as I stated before, even a 'madman' loves someone or something.

Therefore, as you move through your new day—or are coming to the end of your evening—contemplate for a short while on your thoughts and words, and deeds. Were you tolerant? Could you have been more patient with a colleague, friend, or a family member or pet? In time, by considering the purpose of your daily life, you will become more focused upon 'service' to humanity and all life. 'All serve … serve all,' Sai Baba used to say.

The merits of serving others far outweigh the so-called hardship. When you link heart and hands, you connect like daisy chains, once scattered across an imaginary lawn of time, space and all creation. The strength of these connections lies deep inside you, with a real desire to emit love and peace. Your 'bodies', like the stems, may be weak and frail when split open, but when entwined, love flows from one to another. Unlike this chain of 'flowers'—though some call them 'weeds'—the soul is your true connection to me. This can never be broken or pulled apart. You cannot wither, fade, or die.

Furthermore, I see each spark of divinity as myself; hence you are me, as I am you. Keep this knowledge forever in your heart, for it will instil the determination to overcome the daily 'tests' you face. Try to believe all circumstances are blessings, and though they often appear to frustrate, aggravate, annoy, and tease you, it is only the 'monkey' mind becoming irritated, reflecting this consciously upon your thoughts and feelings.

Ignorance of such can be bliss, so go with the flow as much as you can, in the knowledge I am forever watching over you, looking out for you. I wish you only what your heart desires in truth, and not what the mind believes or thinks it needs.

Appreciate there is always someone, somewhere who you could say is 'worse off'. I do not state this to make you feel somewhat better about yourself, but to inspire greater courage within you, for your own life and road ahead. Remember, you are all on countless different paths, and yet embark on the same journey, in order to recognize the true 'you' … and me.

I am not hiding away, deep in a forest or a secluded mountain cave. I am not within the ground, buried as a secret treasure, lost for all time. I am not upon the seabed either, drifting back and forth like the currents of the ocean. No, I am inside your heart. Therefore, you hold, nourish, and sustain me too, while keeping me safe … though many do not realise it.

As I am all things and all things I am, sense and know me in every tree, leaf, rock, blade of grass, flower, the air you breathe, the food and water you consume, the stars, planets, moons, and all creation. If you can trust me on this, then you will trust in yourself. If you can believe that I am and can do what I say, your life will become 'lighter', like floating upon still waters … buoyant, uplifted, and sustained forever in my heart.

Understand, your soul, carried in the vessel called the 'body', has only one true name. This is 'Atma' … 'I am I', or like the clue at the end of a previous lesson, known simply as, 'Me, Myself and I'. Amen.

LESSON 46:

WINTER

As the wind outside howls around your windows and doors, I welcome you to feel the warmth and sustenance 'within'. Here, you will find peace, contentment, and the answers you seek.

For many, the approach of the year-end is fast and furious … just like the gales, which seem to throw you off balance as you walk through your journey called life. Similarly, there are those who believe what they are going through has culminated into a 'winter of discontent', with fear and anguish prominent in both hearts and minds.

"Will I still be at work in 6-or 12-months' time? How can I find the money for Christmas? What will the future hold for me? Surely, next year must be better?" Well, no wonder illness, stress, and disease continually escalate and surface from those unknown depths of one's own shadow of illusion and confusion.

I appreciate how someone with good health, or without financial or family concerns can state, "Just get on with it" or to say one must simply, "Rise above their so-called problems and fears". In contrast, others may wish to offer guidance and support to those who 'suffer' and state, "I can understand what you are going through". However, unless one experiences the same conditions resulting in identical outcomes, this is untrue.

Of course, as pleasing as it is to empathize, sympathize and try to impart wisdom, a far greater importance for those who imagine they are entrapped by 'winter blues', anxiety, and trepidation, is to receive your love … which shines from your heart. Therefore, one must accept the mind, through its own weakness, will occasionally attempt to inflict burdens upon a soul. If left unchecked or isolated by so-called friends or loved ones, this makes the person feel stripped bare and exposed … like a tree, devoid of leaves or bark.

Please comprehend, any being or element of life—without the wisdom of who, what, or why they exist—can become more vulnerable. They believe they are separated or alone, and in trying to weather their own storm of emotions, may reach a breaking point.

Mentally, they can snap. Impulses of the mind's 'consciousness' to the brain shear off. These resemble twigs, then large branches, which break under the pressure, falling away to hit the ground. Left unattended, the body suffers the most. Over time, this can be prolonged … by the denial of self, or by being cast aside, ignored by the bonds and ties of either blood or water. Eventually, they can crack because of the unbearable strain, sensing only one way out, succumbing to self-neglect or instigating a moment of no return.

As one reads—or hears—this, many I's (and eyes) may view these words in a different light. They become illuminated by what they must achieve, or at least start attempting to integrate truth into one's life. Others will have a slower inkling of what direction they are headed, but even though all paths are each your own, you are never alone, as I keep reiterating to every one of you.

People often assume they are taking part in a worthless job. Or, by working in dirty or difficult conditions, they are less important than those who appear to be at the top of the 'tree'—but this makes no difference to me. You must therefore appreciate your own self-worth, because as souls and hearts of love, you are all precious beyond compare. I love you. So, please realise those imagined obstacles and tasks to overcome actually help you develop your character, personality, and should strengthen you, too.

During one's life, if you cannot open your heart and talk to someone else, become 'still'. You can confide in me, in the knowledge I shall not turn you away. I know you better than you can ever know yourself, and am never ashamed of whom, what and why you 'are'. I understand you and will help and guide you, as I love you for all eternity.

Forever your friend and confidant, I am your rock to cling to when all else seems lost around you. I am the light within the darkness, and the helping hand to lift you off the ground when you fall to your knees. I will quench your thirst for knowledge and lead you to the wisdom you need There is always an answer; a way out of the debris and fallout when the emotional storm appears to engulf you in your life.

Appreciate that in all religions and faiths, I am one God. I am love. Nowhere is it written you should hurt or kill. Throughout the eons of time, so many souls believe in their own division from me, igniting karmic imbalance, fuelling desire and inhumane qualities. They resemble dry autumn leaves burning in a woodland fire. These cause rising embers to fly into the air and ether, effectively landing in distant places, spreading like a plague of ill thoughts and deeds towards other hearts.

So, it is imperative to elevate oneself above anxiety and fear, as negativity can spiral out of control. Realise too, in the far reaches and depths of one's own despair lies a monster called depression. Being aware of these offers a chink of light. This enables you to hang onto truth and hope, and be ready to fight your own inner demons of self-doubt and self-worth.

For those close by, sometimes the signs of this appear invisible, even to a best friend, husband, wife, partner, or lover. The tracks and traces often disappear, like footprints in the snow, being erased and covered over by a fresh flurry from above. Throughout your life, it is vital you discover both strength and inspiration. No matter how or where you find them (as long as it is through truth), those dark clouds will fade, turbulent times and situations will ease—which calm you down—and new light will guide you. No longer shall you walk in your own shadow, as this will become a distant memory behind you.

So, how are you now? Well, only you can answer this, but what is important is that you can find your own truth and joy inside you. Whatever thoughts are emanating deep within your heart, they act like a mirror, reflecting way beyond the world in which you live.

In fact, everything is cause and effect., and one can attract so much positive energy by being so. Conversely, negativity combines both fear and dread. Do not misinterpret fate with hate, or life as only light, because one has to bear and love all seasons, all colours of man and the so-called 'good and bad' times with equanimity, too. If I am in you, I am in all things. If you accept this, then surely your acceptance of each other can be the same.

Remember, the sun—and Son—will always rise somewhere upon the Earth. Love always rises to the surface of your heart when you let your smile, handshake, and every thought and word and deed be the reflection from oneself to simply 'self'. Try then to believe the chill of negative times is a mirage. May each day bring a warm glow to radiate through your kindness and laughter forever and a day. In doing so, you will discover your true power, and therefore find me. Amen.

LESSON 47:

FROST

Welcome to thy peace, stillness, and warmth of my loving heart once more. Now, as the outside temperature drops, bringing forth a winter's chill, it enables you to experience the first real frost of the season. With it, a crisp veil of ice has formed. It resembles a carpet of silver and white glitter, and everything around you is being transformed—as if by magic—and nothing escapes its vice like grip.

You gaze upon it, so why not venture outside, and try something new? Perhaps you could walk barefoot on the lawn? If you do, the coolness may shock your feet at first, but sensations rising through you will make you feel truly alive. You will also hear those tiny sound vibrations as your weight squashes the icy particles below you, and these echo and reverberate over many levels.

So too, as the coldness is recognized, and the realization hits your brain, it instantaneously alerts you to this drastic change in temperature. Then, once you leave the grass, the exact opposite occurs. Your feet respond from the numbness, you will certainly become alert and uplifted.

In comparison, how often do you bare your sole(s)/soul to sudden changes in your surroundings? What conditions are you prepared to be exposed to? And just like the frosty lawn, would you undertake these willingly to experiencing the rawness, and for your heart to become immersed in new challenges and ways of being?

Only you can determine and answer such things. But be honest with yourself as you endeavour to walk upon your own road or path. Then, when it is time for you to 'cross over', there is no need to pause, reflect or wish for a chance to turn back the clock … because of regrets, or a desire to erase those doubts of so-called missed opportunities.

To do so is like viewing your steps left behind in the frosted lawn. They may appear to resemble real tracks—a residue of where you have been—but unless you walk in, through, from, and to love, the experiences will eventually fade. Those footprints soon melt away when the sun (and Son) rises above you.

How can you leave a more permanent legacy? What reminder, what memory and treasure can you store within friends, family, and neighbour's hearts and minds? You cannot find the answer in your home, car or the possessions you accumulate upon the Earth. No. Only your love is real and eternal, which is portrayed through one's character and personality.

As I explained many times before, try to be self-less, not selfish. Live with those true human qualities such as truth, non-violence, and righteousness. I do not command or require you to be anything other than what you already are. Only by understanding and knowing your real self ... will you reflect your own divinity.

Therefore, with your day now in motion, what choices did you make? Have you earmarked all your time to embark upon one's toils? Or can you set aside a moment for you, me, and us? Remember, one cannot, or should not, underestimate the moments spent within peace and reflection, especially in the era of such a fast-paced and demanding society of which you are all part. Indeed, remain in the world, but do not believe you are what the world is, separated from your true self and me.

Moving on from this, one's environment can appear dull and withered during winter, so it is prudent to view through different lenses. Unlike those three-dimensional (3D) glasses, which attempt to imitate real life on a television screen, please look and feel with your heart instead. This will bring new and pleasant surprises every day. For instance, birds still fly and sing, while a tree—even without leaves—draws one to the beauty of its bark. Also, when conditions are exactly right, a full moon in the coldness of night will cause the rooftops to shimmer and shine like mirrors ... while hedgerows and verges sparkle like stardust, as car headlights compete with nature's rays of light.

One must realise, as you make your way through the journey of your life and soul, there are those whose hearts are frozen. Coming across individuals or groups of people with chilled emotions may often prove difficult. Therefore, please see these not as obstacles or challenges, but fresh opportunities to melt hardened feelings with kindness and gratitude.

Others can be difficult to talk to, work alongside, or even become friends with. They resemble hearts coated in candy sugar. They are both very sweet and nice, but under this exterior layer—deep inside—lurks anger, frustration, and many fears. On the other hand, if the heart is plainly good and a joy to be near, the thin protective shield surrounding it, may wish to stop many emotions, thoughts, and feelings from entering, and as such prefers a self-imposed solitude upon itself.

Be delicate. Tread carefully when interacting with a heart like this. Some are so fragile from their own grief or pain, or from living in their own struggle to make sense of life and the world, that one sharp word, action or thought, can crack the ice, penetrating deep within.

Please refrain from attempting to break this too soon. Do not force attitudes or beliefs on another, as all life must keep the choice of whom, what or why they believe in someone or something. Indeed, they may require gently thawing instead, so their own development can flourish like a flower bulb, peering through the surface of the ground as and when spring appears. In fact, why not ask yourself, "Am I prepared? Do I wish to learn and grow within and 'without' this mortal coil?"

Well, just like an overcoat—which tries to protect you from the cold—the body wants to adjust and adapt to its different situations and conditions it finds itself in. Too hot and you will sweat. The body releases what it doesn't need, but the soul also wishes to attain balance, removing karmic debt where it can, so the overcoat or 'body' will no longer be required either. Do not think in terms of becoming exposed. Rather, you are a living, burning flame of immense strength, enabling other hands and souls to find you for healing, direction, and purpose.

For this reason, know my love 'lights' the way for you when all other lights dim or fade away. Remember, the frost is but a temporary condition. So now move forward in the knowledge both warmth and comfort are only a heartbeat away. Amen.

LESSON 48:

HISTORY

The physical heart of your body beats like a drum—many times per minute —but the flame and radiating coil at the seat of your soul resonates many more per second. In a similar fashion, this life-giving organ enables your blood to be cleansed and circulated around the body. It brings vital protection and nutrients to every fibre, sinew, muscle, and veins. Meanwhile, the illumination of love from your spark of divinity provides power as it flows and pulses with beams of energy so finite, only the vision of body, mind, and soul in unison can see it.

Like a mirror, this reflects from both the inside and out. Therefore, everyone notices when their body 'surface' changes—as if you are wearing different clothes throughout the seasons of one's life—whether that's during childhood, your youth, and teenage years, and into middle and old age. The inner flame, however, reflects true character and personality, along with the knowledge, experience, and wisdom of the soul, through every thought, word, and deed, but who can comprehend this?

How many of you recognize your own traits and qualities, or dare I say, perhaps your own faults, too? In addition, at what point would one realise the consequences of their actions, which affect those far beyond the walls in which they live?

Often, someone will think they can do no wrong, but on the other hand, one may feel they can do no right either! Well, I can help you then, by asking you to imagine you had a two-way mirror, so you could see in a different light. You could even demand to know what is real, or are you guilty of something which you can only ever ask of yourself?

As you are your own judge and jury, this is your own decision to make. What is more intriguing occurs in the recognition of such, since it allows you to access reality, which enables you to question the 'confined', the informant, the 'one' who is held until the truth 'will out'.

Please comprehend it is 'I' who am your captive ... or that I am 'captivated' by your essence and the power of your love. I am a 'model' prisoner, though, because I serve you freely, wantonly, and willingly, without exception.

So, where have I been and where can I go? Well, if I am under a nonphysical lock and key, this can only represent true love and light. Recognize the two co-exist as one, and by that, we can deem them 'unfit for purpose' or are an amazing combination, linked forever into eternity.

Try to create a new scene within your mind and picture this two-way mirror … which now lets you observe me, to state, "You only require the truth, and then you will release me". But will you? Could you free me from your heart, so I can bear witness to the reflection, which shines from all those whom you meet and greet?

Do not get angry or become frustrated with me, either. Those feelings only block out what I am trying to tell you and prevents love from entering your soul, which in turn leads the hands to action. Therefore, you want the truth, the whole truth and nothing but the truth … do you?

"Yes, I do. So where were you?"

I am everywhere.

"Ok, now tell me, what did you take from me?"

I took all your sins.

"Why?"

Well, by clearing your karma, you find balance. When you obtain balance, you will discover contentment and peace. Recognizing peace through 'self-realization', you enter bliss. Once here, you appreciate you are truly 'home' … forever beside, within, without, above, and below me.

"I hear what you're saying, God, but that's just part of history, right?"

No, that's 'His-Story' … the way, the truth, and the light.

"How can I believe you … that what you are telling me is true?"

What other proof do you need—or want?

"Maybe we all want a miracle. Yes, that's it … we do! We need something we can all witness with our own eyes, and not what happened in texts of old within lots of different religions and faiths around the

world."

You are 'it'.

"What's that supposed to mean?"

You are the miracle.

"Eh? I'm confused."

Do not be. Now you're taking off the rose-coloured spectacles, you can re-focus through the lens of your heart, because you know I exist.

"I do?"

Of course ... we're both talking, aren't we?

"Oh, but how do I know it's not all a trick?"

Why would I do that, you are the one with the key, remember?

"Alright, so the miracle is 'I'?"

Yes. For you neither recognized your true self, nor the power inside you. Please comprehend, this allows you to choose not only to live, but to love and shine, too. How else can you keep me hidden for so long?

"Okay, okay, okay. So, what you are saying then, is you're the innocent one in all this?"

No, not at all ... only that guilt and blame hold no place in your heart, and because you were not living the truth, by acting from—and seeing with—your heart ... you had forgotten who and what you are.

"And that is?"

That you are already 'free'. Please remember, all the while you believed it is I, fighting to break out, but I wasn't. You imagined the body was all there is, hence, you were trapping your own 'self'. In doing so, you could not sense me.

"In fact, I can't even recall how I got you in here, so I could ask you these things."

I was here before you even 'existed' ... for I was, am and forever will be, and now you will be too.

"I'm beginning to understand. You are love ... and I am too, right?"

Of course.

"So, what do I do now?"

Release me. It must be you who sets me free in order to let me work through you and your heart.

"Will I need to change anything?"

Only your thoughts, as they often hold you back. Think, and then feel, share, be, and act from and through and to love. You might find this difficult at first, but you will learn from any mistakes ... so do not fear, because any consequences will be my burden if you try to live in truth.

"Huh, you've just handed me a 'get out of jail free' card!"

No, it is you who gives it to me.

"Thank you, God. I will need to write this into the record book now, as anyone else who brings you in for questioning can save time and effort ... the truth written for all to see."

Indeed, that may help many.

"What do you want me to do now?"

I do not need or want you to do anything ... other than to be your actual self. You are the miracle, remember. Believe in yourself and make your life a happy one by making your dreams come true. I am working with, through, in, and from you, as I have always tried to do.

The only difference is that you now comprehend us as 'one'. The false separation of the two needed to be dispelled, especially when the heart has yearned for more than everyday life, much more than just eating, working, and sleeping. In recognizing there was—and is—more to life than yourself, you'll know what is real, bringing history and 'His-Story' of the past, through to the present, and for a bright new future.

Realise we are connected by chains of love and light, and those magical cords of truth, into eternity. Therefore, be who you were born to be and do not waste time and become fulfilled in the knowledge you are already free.

Illuminate and shine all you are and can be from 'within'. Before long, others will remember their own reality and understand their own 'history' to reveal my gift, which I pre-sent to carry you every day, through the future, and throughout the eons of time. Amen.

LESSON 49:

GARLAND

Like so many places on the Earth—and indeed throughout creation—I welcome you by placing a garland of beautiful flowers around your neck. To you, it is similar to a radiant rainbow … but this is vastly different. The petals open wide to the light, resonating from and through and to your heart, and every plume represents truth, love, and hope.

I pre-sent, and now present, this to be adorned by you all—with strength, conviction, perseverance, gratitude, and contentment. So, who will witness these attributes? Who can sense they are bestowed with such a gift? Well, as each body and soul receive it with my grace, only you can answer this question alone. Like karma, no one can erase, accrue, or inflict further imbalance upon anyone else. You all have your own choices to make, and lives to fulfil.

Please understand, the flowers of the garland resemble your souls, connected by an invisible thread of truth. In fact, this is pure, divine, and permanently attached to me … unlike the umbilical cord cut away at birth— or re-birth—separating the body from the mother. No, what I speak of sustains and provides you with everything you need to survive and grow … like a baby in a womb. However, this also carries eternal love, truth, and every ingredient one can think of … and the knowledge of who and what you are deep inside your heart and soul, too.

For many, though, they still imagine isolation, as if divided from me. All must realise … no garland—containing only one flower or symbol—exists to represent division. Nor placed over you upon your arrival in paradise.

Please comprehend the glory of the truth was with you in the beginning, and perpetually stay through you whenever and wherever you reside. Time, distance, levels of vibration or dimension make no difference either. Love is whole. It is universal and all powerful, and forms creation itself. It is not just for the 'Son' but is for everyone. All you need to do is to recognize this through the realization of the self … by remembering and becoming who and what you truly are.

This is the only truth which can be imparted to you in any form or means you can understand. It does not matter where or when you were born into the physical, because colour, creed, and religion bear no effect on your soul.

Everything else is for each heart to process when the correct time in your life materializes. Therefore, someone else's truth and experiences may not resonate inside you. Explanations and their own 'reasoning' are more varied and countless, like the grains of sands on every shore, or the stars glistening within the depths of night.

Perhaps you can regard these latest threads as the web of life, a template or blueprint, but ultimately, even these must be digested and acted upon by your own heart. The outcome should be the same. It will lead you into bliss and peace, but this is—and remains—your choice.

When truth is revealed, connecting directly with your soul, you will know and feel it, like a hand in a glove or your feet in well-worn shoes. This is because you have the instant recognition. They belong to you and you to them. They are a perfect fit, comfortable, without resistance or restriction, which brings the sense of wholeness.

Compare this, for example, to a pair of boots, two sizes too small. You would experience pain ... dis-'ease', and immense pressure to persevere and continue wearing them. True spiritual education and guidance are never like this. In contrast, imagine they were way too big. Your balance turns to imbalance, and you will slip and slide about, perhaps even stumble, falling awkwardly to the floor. Truth does not teach this way. So, only you can decide what feels real and ready to be taken on board by your body, mind, and soul.

Of course, there will be those who do not even believe in themselves, and so they cannot acknowledge me either. Perhaps they see the garland of my love in a different light, carrying their own anchor (anger), around their necks, which weighs them down, routing them to the spot. Remember, it is your decision on how you 'see' such things in your life. This has a massive bearing upon events, opportunities, and experiences.

So, do you see your glass half full or half empty? This analogy in its simplest form shows one's thoughts have a major impact on daily life. As this is so, learning to train any wayward or monkey mind is crucial. When a negative thought enters your consciousness, try to override it as soon as possible. Counteract it with positive feelings, picturing an outcome of joy, love, and hope ... away from fear, hate, and helplessness.

By recognizing those moments when something bizarre flies into your mind—generating anxiety or stress—it is important to ignore them quickly, and in time, this process becomes easier. The opposite occurs only if we leave negativity to take hold, like a seed which somehow grows upon the infertile ground, yet still flourishes to become a weed. This nuisance must not be allowed to grow. Attempt to pluck and remove them at the earliest opportunity.

One must realise some of your negative thoughts are deep-rooted, and in turn, they take a greater effort to erase. Please try, otherwise they can spread, touching, and taking over others, because your concerns and worries are naturally 'shared' with your family or friends.

Like a common cold, the germination of a virus is quick, does not discriminate over young or old, colour or creed; it only wants to multiply and extend itself. The difference now, though, is that you know you have the choice, a real weapon in your armoury of defence. Let this knowledge be your shield. It will protect you, bringing strength and fortitude over many minor irritations, but even more so, if the roller-coaster of life hits a new low.

Without doubt, you can ride out the troughs and elevate to new heights of experience and happiness, so when all is said and done, try to live your life in joy. I know this can be difficult at times, and you may think it's not much fun or even fair … which begs the question of how anyone would call the Earth—or life—a 'playground'.

However, the inner connection to each other is eternal, and the garland of my grace you wear will keep you away from all despair … if you let it! Though I placed this around your neck, it actually rests over your heart. So, reach for it, symbolically, with both hands, to enable your mind, body, and soul to ride those ups and downs with ease. Please enjoy this experience of so-called 'life', as it is freely given to you … to succeed through love forever. Amen.

LESSON 50:

CLUTTER

I am fully aware you know I am here. So welcome to your recognition and connection to our love once more. As you go through your earthbound and physical day, thinking, working, and trying to sustain yourself and your family, one cannot help but see complexity … instead of simplicity. Sometimes the mind is in such a rush to contemplate, workout, and work through its thoughts, wishes, and deeds, but how many of these are truly required? Do you recognize when 'desire' is influencing your life, which affects those around you, too?

It can be difficult to wade through these matters, as if walking across a desert dune, a sodden field, or worse still, shallow pools of quicksand, as they all attempt to hold and bind you in place. In fact, when one finds oneself in this situation of anxiety and stress, you're sapped of energy, becoming physically, mentally, and emotionally drained.

Please understand, the mind can also bring chaos if left to its own devices and desires. This leads to irrational speech and behaviour. Like tentacles, they try to suck others into the same mire of so-called illusion and confusion. Crucially, one must de-clutter the debris of irritations and trivialities, which endeavours to weave their way into your daily life. Before they can take hold, release the feelings of attachment, in what you falsely sense as being critical to your survival, accumulating what is irrelevant to the body, soul, or heart.

Imagine the scenario of a friend or family member having possessions they no longer need, or that you see material things in a bin, or even items on someone's doorstep with a note, 'free to a good home'. Would you think you actually require them or take them just for the sake of it? Do you desire more 'stuff'? If so, why?

Does the mind tell you this, while imposing a rush of blood to the head? At times like these, stop what you are doing and feel from the heart. Then, simply ask yourself, "For what purpose is this happening? Will it sustain and improve my life, or the well-being of those around me?"

Remember, one can live in a mansion, but you can only fall asleep in one bed. Some, though, assume bigger is better. This is fine, as long as worthwhile, and true reasons exist behind those thoughts and wishes. It is important, therefore, to remove attachment, wherever and whenever possible, in all that's said and done. This becomes simple when one loses the sense of a 'what is mine is mine' attitude or syndrome. By becoming detached emotionally from the material elements of the impermanent world, an easier road lies ahead.

If you can change your thought process, the clutter you collect along the way—in so many aspects of your life—will lose their importance. This enables a clearer passage for your happiness and wellbeing. Of course, I appreciate many people state 'one man's rubbish is another man's treasure', and that 'one day, it might come in handy' … perhaps something will, or maybe it won't.

These statements and traits can be linked to the fear of not having 'enough'. Or one might think it could 'save money in the long run', which is all well and good, but in the meantime, your surroundings remain clogged, with less space for you to move and just 'be'.

In this case, one day you may realise 'you cannot see the 'wood for the trees'. Then, different feelings of frustration, anxiety or even anger can rear their ugly head. The mind and one's health suffer from this conflict within, which affects those close by, such as family and friends, too.

One must comprehend, this is not always about attraction, but detaching the elements which try to cling or hang on to your heartstrings. Retaining gratitude for what one already has leads to appreciation and contentment. Attachment carries the dread of 'losing', leading to worry, anguish and dis-'ease'.

Due to all your different characters, personalities, and responsibilities, I understand one's hobbies are an outlet, releasing a pressure valve, or even a form of escapism for so many of you. We often connect these with sports, nature or even in the materialistic sense, whereby you collect something. You name it … stamps, music, books, pictures, ornaments, thimbles or toys, and someone, somewhere, has a fascination and needs to store or accumulate it.

Why do this? Is it wrong, or right? Well, everything carries a reason for each one of you. Remember, all you do must be good for yourself and society. So, does it harm or propose any forms of conflict to oneself or another? If you gave it up or stop right now, what thoughts do they trigger deep within you? Inside, you'll know the answer!

Whatever you do, realise by clearing and removing any clutter—on any level of your being you can think of—will create 'space' … yes, room for both the true you, and 'us'. Perhaps new ways of thinking and being, and new opportunities can finally flow to and through you without certain aspects of your current life getting in the way. How good would this make you feel?

In addition, so many people and 'things' in your life will come and go, like the ever-flowing ebb of tides upon the Earth. So too, your emotions keep a 'push me - pull you' effect on them, through your everyday choices, concerns, attitudes, and so-called happy and sad times. Remember, the only thing you need is love, and to love 'self', each other, and all life.

Appreciate your possessions may indeed become a cause and trigger of a memory, but ultimately, whatever touches your heart needs no actual physical reminder. Love is the only permanent issue here, and this one truth shines above all transient elements in every dimension, time and space which has ... or ever will ... exist.

It cannot be boxed and stored away in a shed, garage, or attic. Nor can it be destroyed by fire, be buried, or disappear into the ether, although time can appear to make the 'need' and link seem to fade. But true love is the jewel in our crown, for it radiates, resonates, and never dissipates. You can find this, I promise you! Like a needle in a haystack of concern and trepidation, the beautiful plumes, and petals of a single flower amongst the weeds growing in barren soil, or a four-leaf clover seemingly disguised within countless of its kind.

Try to remove sentiment, for like cement, it attempts to bind you. In doing so, the false attachment is removed and 'sent to me' instead. I retain it as my burden and not your own, because you no longer need to rely on it. You will feel freer within your life; this I assure you.

All that is required for you to do ... is to decide where and when you will start. Is it in the mind, the heart, or in the very room in which you read or hear these words? Appreciate I am always with you, so even if you believe certain aspects of truth are difficult to achieve, lean on me. Ask me to help you move forward, and I will give you strength to accomplish what you must complete. Just believe and trust in yourself too, for you can make the changes you need in your life.

When all is said and done, everyone must accept their most prized possession—the physical body—has been removed ... but will soon appreciate they are left with the perfection of light, love, and soul. Through self-realization, you can attain pure bliss and peace and know the true removal of clutter. Amen.

LESSON 51:

IMMORTALITY

To every heart and soul and element of life throughout creation, I welcome thee for guidance, truth, and love. Please understand, though, even with knowledge and wisdom gained through this book, and in all sacred texts or scriptures over the eons of time, there are additional meanings—some say they are hidden—to learn and digest. So too, with the title of this lesson, for you could easily read this as 'I'm More Totality'.

Therefore, if you do, would you then believe this refers to me (I am I); yourself, or us both … not as separate individuals, beings, or elements …but as one light? At first, some of you may find this a difficult concept to accept. Over time, by connecting with your heart and reaching the stillness inside, it will become easier until self-realization is your own reality.

However, over the ages, 'man' has sought riches and sustenance in almost every way possible upon the impermanent world in which you now live. Originally, he searched high and low and far and wide for the holy grail of divinity and true longevity. Instead—and for such a long while into this modern age—'he' now speaks and seeks the immortality of the physical body. Why is this? And for what purpose, too?

Imagine if you could live forever within the same shell, your current overcoat of the soul … how old would you prefer to be? And would you still wish for this if you were destitute and homeless, or currently starving and desperately needing to quench your thirst too? On the other side of the coin, if you were rich and famous, at what point can you honestly say you would go ahead? Think long and hard about this and ask yourself if you could live with the consequences … if it came true.

One must appreciate, as friends, family, and loved ones pass through the stages of life, their bodies will eventually turn to dust and decay … while your attachment to your own can only generate a painful separation. Tears will fall, as a companion after companion takes flight into the light. Here, the danger of drowning in your own pool of self-inflicted loneliness becomes the new reality. But then you wouldn't drown at all because you would constantly try to reach the shore of peace and tranquillity … which seems to shine a false horizon of unfulfilled hopes and dreams of your soul.

In essence, what do you really need to do? What is the real destination of your heart, soul, and real immortality? Well, as I stated frequently before, you must first lose your immorality and become a true being of human values—radiating kindness, compassion, love, forgiveness, and truth. These are the stepping-stones across the waters of doubt and fear. They guide you toward my eternal heart. The immortality of the soul is the reality, but it is in the recognition and understanding of such which leads you towards the goal.

If you can, try to imagine you're in a severe snowstorm or blizzard. The wind is so strong it almost blows you off your feet. Now think from the heart, for you cannot look forward when you become blinded by the hail of illusion called deceit, lies, and fears. These constantly pressure your mind, leading you astray, off track, and away from your intended destination.

To the right, you somehow visualise what looks like a rope, fixed above the ground. By attaching yourself to this guide of trust, faith, perseverance, and fortitude, you can now re-begin the pathway once more. Indeed, you have tried many times before—perhaps in numerous incarnations—only to struggle and lose your way. Not this time. The rope is my cord and our connection. In fact, it's always been there, but until you truly searched, you assumed it wasn't there. Even through your constant efforts, it was as if it was out of sight and out of mind.

So, you can now forge ahead. Each step brings you closer to realising you are only returning to yourself, coming full circle—totality. I hope this now registers within your heart that you are both the journey and the destination. By following the path and thread of truth, you will enjoy the 'bliss', and ultimately find peace and rest away from the blizzard, forevermore.

Remember, you all possess the ability to assist your fellow souls in seeking this, too. Appreciate, however, you can only help and guide, as not one 'step' can be taken by you on behalf of another. Everyone lives with their own tasks to complete. Self-realization only comes through one's own efforts to gain it.

Within every truthful aspect of this 'earth-plane', no exam, test or challenge can be passed without effort to reshape the memory and the mind. Thorough and correct training—and perseverance—are required. It would be like trying to climb Mount Everest, without acclimatizing at base camp first. Even a desire to achieve does not attain your goal … unless you practice and work your way through the 'experience' itself.

So, once you comprehend that I am I, the Indweller of your Heart, there is no turning back. This is not because I can prevent you from doing so, but because you will not want to! Everything worth having is worth fighting for, right? With the support of the heavenly realms of both love and light, and through your own endeavours, you can—and will—succeed.

One must understand that mistakes may be made, too. But know those times of weakness can be good if you learn from them. Reliving, or rather remaking past errors not so, as this only shows a lack of concentration, which then leads to questioning your own determination and attitude towards the tasks in front of you.

At some point, you will experience a clearing of the sky—or in this case, your mind. The driving ice and snow, which had bound and blinded you, will cease. Hence, the road ahead becomes more manageable, as those peaks and troughs of your journey are seen with true insight instead.

Please comprehend, your real heart mirrors mine, made of the divine essence called love. Everything else you see is a wrapping, which hides and disguises the 'higher self'. This is why so many of you think you are different, but you are not.

The dialect of many tongues, the colours of skin, gender, and your shapes and sizes, all show dissimilarities, but love is the one thing which unites you all: every creature, being, energy, and soul. Know it is the ultimate power, and the universal language of the heart needs no words.

Remember, love flows from, through, and to all 'life' … and in fact, cannot be destroyed by time, distance, or any dimension. As this is so, you are the same too. You are already immortal inside my heart, and forever sustained within my name. Amen.

LESSON 52:

DIAMONDS

I welcome you all to the last lesson of the year, but by no means is it the end of love, light, and truth. Even though there are now many lessons to draw upon, many souls wish for further help and advice in the form of the written word. The where and the when, of course, will become known in good time, and for the 'pen' to communicate spiritual guidance, education, and wisdom from, through, and to the heart once more.

So, as each lesson becomes etched in your mind and relayed deep within you, what prevents these words from disappearing into the ether or fading from memory? Surely, such messages being conveyed with ink can only lighten and grow fainter over time?

Well, the truth is different. This is being written with permanence, like a diamond upon granite. You see, for something to be real and tangible, and become pure inside you, unless it resonates with simplicity, it would be like chalk on pavements, washed away by the emotional tears which rain down from thy heart. Similarly, with text, when written into the sands of time, it can be easily erased by the winds of change.

Please appreciate love flows like light. It can travel through a diamond, unhindered by the denseness of the world in which you live. In fact, this is a prized jewel. Its unique qualities make it a valuable and true 'currency' where your physical resides.

Likewise, every human being and soul are precious. And beyond priceless. You are each a living flame and an expression of me, forming the crown of my heart. Indeed, you are all the embodiment of my love. As divinity personified, billions of you—and every being too—cannot say one is worth more than another, or indeed greater than anything else.

In reality, whether rich, poor, meek, or mild; and if one is white, yellow, red, or black, you just have different facets, shapes, sizes, characters, and personalities which make you unique. Your karma may reflect your imperfections, those chips, dents, and scratches caused only by—and to— each other. A diamond can only affect another, and vice versa, remember.

Your own thoughts, words, and deeds make all limitations. No intervening hand creates them to inflict pain or hardship, or by making some feel less worthy, unloved, or alone. No, only truth is highlighted and

179

revealed as waves and beams of light. Someone cannot manipulate or disguise these, like throwing a wet blanket over flames, snuffing out a candle, or by flicking a switch to off.

Comprehend the term 'do not fear when I am near', because love always finds a way through the shadows of illusion and confusion. Likewise, we both have the same goal, which is to smooth out and erase any exterior imperfections of hate, anger, jealousy, and ego. Your inner search for peace, bliss, and self-realization then becomes much easier to materialize and achieve.

One may sometimes think that this—or I—am hard to find, but how often would you find a precious jewel just sitting there on the ground? Please understand, by turning within to the stillness and peace, you are digging below the surface, searching towards the light at the end of the tunnel. With perseverance, stamina, and determination—combined with positive thoughts and words and deeds—I guarantee you will succeed. Everything worth having is more satisfying if attained this way, is it not? Remember, I am with you. If you trust in me, letting me work through you … then you cannot fail.

In terms of divinity, I am the expression of love, for no soul was ever born with a silver spoon in its mouth. In fact, firstly you were never born at all, but were already part of me. Second, every single spark of light has developed themselves through experience and knowledge, bringing wisdom from deep within.

Like film inside an old camera, one can stay seemingly—and falsely—contained in its casement … called the 'body'. The flash—light—of the mind only illuminates the truth when it is ready to, which deceives many into thinking the world is full of shadow and doubt when it is not. Therefore, the negativity needs to be transformed through this pretend and so-called darkened room of—and upon—Earth to reveal the picture of truth.

Once exposed, the mind, heart, and soul—in unison—can bear witness to the glory of our love. The pieces of one's life—like a jigsaw puzzle discussed once before—shall come together. Then you can then frame this (to be displayed) for all to view who, what, and why you truly are divine.

Some of you take time to develop, like the images of 'old'. Others may resemble and be like a digital camera, revealing an image or scene almost instantaneously to be viewed by one's 'self' or by another. Imagine if a photograph were taken of you right now, how would that make you feel? Is your hair, okay? Do you think you ought to change how you dress and look? What sort of makeover do you think would make you happy, and more content? And if so, who are you then trying to please? Is it the photographer, perhaps your friends or family, even strangers … or is it for yourself?

Everything comes from within, but your face becomes a canvass, displaying and radiating love or hate … as your smile or frown can elevate or cause a debate. Know that while technology can disguise and manipulate those tracks of your tears from red eyes … they cannot be hidden from me. Therefore, I understand and know you, and moreover, of what you need, when you need it, and why.

I hope you try to be yourself, and happy in your own skin. Through thick and thin, hold on to your own beliefs and faith if they are true. Be able to look in the mirror, accept, and like what you see. Let everything you say, think and do be the real reflection of your own heart … and not what someone else thinks what they wish to see, or for you to be.

In all relationships, there is give and take. There may be compromise and forgiveness, gratitude and understanding, but that gives no other person the right to treat another as a doormat, by leaving their unwanted feelings or traits at someone else's door.

Okay, it is now time to close once more, but I ask every soul and spark of divinity to shine and reflect their love towards, through, and from each other. Be polished in all that's said and done … not covered by dust, dirt, or debris, falsely disguised by the impermanent world around you.

I love you. I believe in you. If I could desire or perhaps wish anything for you all, it would be for you to recognize and become your own love … which eternally abides and lives in every heart and soul. Amen.

CONCLUSION

You and I are 'one'. So, if you are the 'wave', you can never become separated or divided from me upon this ocean called love. Therefore, if you are still searching across the false sea of 'illusion'—which is being subjected through and across your mind—what additional proof do you then need? And where can you find the answers that you seek?

As I am in all things, just understand that I am the Indweller of your heart —and then you will remember me. I do not ask you to give up or deny anything in which you already believe. Every faith and all colours, creeds, and languages of man wishes for you to bask in the glory of 'God'.

Know that your path and road ahead will become much easier if you recognize the attachment to your senses. They act like mirrors, reflecting a fog of confusion from the impermanent world in which you live. Therefore, try to clear this mist, not by looking through rose-tinted glasses, but by witnessing and removing the curtains and shadows of doubt before you. You may then witness the truth from and through and 'within' your heart.

By hearing me in the 'stillness' (and with the aid of these new lessons), you realise they are yet another steppingstone to help you through—and across—the emotional waters you call life. By debating, meditating, and reflecting upon them, you discover you are already free. You will soon find your own truth, which is essential to fulfil your destiny. So, keep moving forward … and strive towards your goal of self-realization, into eternal bliss and peace.

FURTHER READING

You will find your own guidance and inspiration every day, week, month, or year as nothing in life is ever by 'chance'. Each lesson will simply be the most appropriate for your needs at that time. They will help you to find inner peace and balance, as well as your own spiritual education, growth and understanding. Here is a selection of my favourite books and authors, which I hope you will enjoy reading too.

Sai Baba Gita-
The Way to Self-Realization and Liberation in this age.
By Al Drucker
ISBN 0-9638449-0-3

Conversations with God
By Neale Donald Walsh
Book 1 - ISBN 0-340-69325-8
Book 2 - ISBN 0-340-76544-5
Book 3 - ISBN 0-340-76545-3

The Message of a Master
By John McDonald
ISBN 0-931432-95-2

The Celestine Prophecy- An Adventure
By James Redfield
ISBN 0-533-40902-6

Anastasia- The Ringing Cedar series -Book 1
By Vladimir Megre
ISBN 978-0-9801812-0-3

A Course in Miracles
By The Foundation for Inner Peace
ISBN 0-670-86975-9

The Winds of Change
By Stephanie J. King
ISBN 978-0954242169

The Day my life changed
By Carmel Reilly
ISBN 978-1-84509-420-1
Confessions of a Pilgrim
Bu Paulo Coelho
ISBN 0-7225-3293-8

A Mind of your Own
By Betty Shine
ISBN 0-00-255894-7

Angel Inspiration
By Diana Cooper
ISBN 0-340-73323-3

Chicken Soup for the Soul
By Jack Canfield and Mark Victor Hansen
ISBN 0-09185-428-8

The Complete Book of Dreams
By Edwin Raphael
ISBN 0-572-01714-6

The Bible Code
By Michael Drosnin
ISBN 0-297-82994-7

Noah Finn & the Art of Suicide
By E. Rachael Hardcastle
ISBN: 978-1999968816

Noah Finn & the Art of Conception
By E. Rachael Hardcastle
ISBN: 978-1999968861

ABOUT THE AUTHOR

David has helped to conduct spiritual development and healing circles for over 25 years. He has also been a guest speaker—sharing his enlightened experiences to promote 'oneness'—at various Mind, Body and Spirit engagements across the UK.

Through inner-dictation, dream interpretation, meditation, mindfulness, pre-cognition, and healing, the books he co-writes with 'Spirit' provide you with the foundation to discover your own path of truth. With a renewed sense of purpose, the spiritual guidance and education you receive can help you reach the goal of self-realization and bliss within the permanence of love and light.

David is tee-total and a vegetarian, who loves the sunshine, nature, animals, and his wife!

INVITATION FROM DAVID KNIGHT

If you enjoyed reading *I AM I The Indweller of Your Heart—Book Two,* you can download *Deliverance of Love, Light and Truth* for free when you join David's mission for a 'full and blissful life'.

To learn more, visit www.AscensionForYou.com

Follow us on

Facebook: facebook.com/ascensionforyou
or
Twitter: https://twitter.com/ascensionforyou

and become part of our community who love to receive uplifting messages for the heart and soul!

Want to let others know what you think? Please make your opinion known by leaving a 'star rating' with one-click on Amazon.com or Amazon.co.uk and/or a review at your favourite online retailer.

Thank you!